Lenten Guidebook

Reflections and Meal-Plans for Every Day of Lent

Sr. Vassa Larin
and Denise Canellos, MS, CNS

XENOPHON PRESS

Title:
HealthyFast Lenten Guidebook: Reflections and Meal-Plans for Every Day of Lent

ISBN: 9781948717403
Copyright © 2021 Sister Vassa Larin.

All rights reserved. No part of this book may be reproduced, stored in a retrieval system, or transmitted in any form or by any means, electronic, mechanical, photocopying, recording, or otherwise, without the prior written permission of the author, except as provided by U.S.A. copyright law.

Published by Xenophon Press LLC
10237 Rogers Drive
Nassawadox Va 23413 USA
XenophonPress@gmail.com
1-757-442-1060

TABLE OF CONTENTS

Foreword..1

Shopping List..3

Nutritional & Fasting Principles of Healthy*Fast*..................................5

Daily Reflections & Fast-Rule for Every Day of the Lenten Season...............10

Meal Plans (**A**), (**B**), (**C**), (**D**), (**E**), and (**F**)......................................87

Recipes...105

      Main Courses & Salads..106

      Dips & Dressings..121

      Desserts & Snacks..123

About the Author..125

Notes..126

Lenten Calendar...130

FOREWORD

Welcome, Healthy*Fast*er!

This program is intended as an aid to busy lay people, who feel ill-equipped to "keep up" with both the liturgical and dietary complexities of the Byzantine tradition(s) for Lent, or find these hard to implement in a healthy manner, but who, nonetheless, would like to re-connect with the faith-based, ancient "wellness"-program that is "The Holy and Great Forty Days" of Lent.

Along with this Guidebook, the Healthy*Fast* program includes **5-days-a-week audio-podcasts called "Morning Coffee,"** hosted by Sister Vassa; a **weekly video** for every week of Lent; and the opportunity for you to leave **your comments/questions**, and to share your Lenten journey with other Healthy*Fast*ers – all on patreon.com/sistervassa. Subscribe to these podcasts and do not hesitate to share your journey, because fasting is teamwork!

In this Lenten Guidebook you will find:

1. A **Lenten Calendar**, showing the liturgical structure of Orthodox Lent, along with the fasting-rule of each day of the Lenten season.

2. A **Shopping List**, to help you stock your pantry and fridge for Lent.

3. The **Nutritional and Fasting Principles** of Healthy*Fast*, by Greek Orthodox certified nutritionist Denise Canellos, MS, CNS. (Find Denise's website at: denisecanellos.com.)

4. **Daily Reflections/Devotions**, written by Sister Vassa, to help you stay focused every day of the liturgical fasting-season called Lent, including the three weeks before, and the one after Lent (Bright Week). Under each reflection is the Fasting Rule or its corresponding **Meal Plan** (see p. 88 of this Guidebook) for the day, classified in this program as (**A**), (**B**), (**C**), (**D**), and (**E**), according to the fasting system of the Sabbaite Typikon.[1]

4. A variety of healthy Fasting and Non-Fasting **Meal-Plans**, prepared in collaboration with certified nutritionist Denise Canellos, MS, CNS.

5. Plenty of simple Healthy*Fast* **Recipes**, prepared by certified nutritionist Denise Canellos, MS, CNS.

May this program be helpful to all of us, Healthy*Fast*ers, as we embark on the Lenten journey together!

---

[1] Please note that the strict oil-free fasting, which this Typikon prescribes for most weekdays (but not weekends) of Lent, is often not practiced by laypeople, and also not in all monasteries. Many faithful, both laypeople and monastics, fast *without entirely abstaining from oil* on weekdays; or some will keep an entirely oil-free fast only for Week 1 of Lent, and also for Great/Holy Week. Healthy*Fast*ers are encouraged to decide on their Lenten fasting-rule with regard to oil before Lent begins; to prepare for it by stocking the pantry and refrigerator accordingly; and then happily to stick to the chosen plan. See more on the **Nutrition & Fasting Principles** of Healthy*Fast* on p. 6 of this Guidebook.

SHOPPING LIST
for a well-stocked Lenten pantry & fridge

Produce
Enough fresh fruit for at least 2 servings a day (recipes here call for Granny Smith apples, watermelon, papaya, berries, pineapple, kiwi, melon)
Avocados
Lemons and limes
Cauliflower
Salad greens, enough for a salad a day per person
2-3 bunches hearty greens - spinach, Swiss chard, kale, etc.
Radishes
Cucumbers (small ones are extra-good in salads)
Tomatoes
Carrots
Celery
Onions (red onions are tasty in salads)
Garlic
Green vegetables (broccoli, green beans, asparagus, Brussels sprouts)
Squash and Eggplant
Bell Peppers
Mushrooms
Sweet and normal potatoes (if watching your weight, avoid the potatoes)
Herbs (parsley, dill, basil, mint)

Frozen
Edamame
Berries
Cooked grains (brown rice, quinoa)
Cauliflower Rice

Grains & Healthy Pasta
Oats for oatmeal, steel cut or Old Fashioned
Buckwheat
Farro
Quinoa
Brown rice
Whole grain bread
Whole wheat, chickpea-flour, or lentil pasta

Dairy Alternatives
Soy, almond, or oat milk (sugar free)
Soy, almond, or coconut yogurt (sugar free)

Legumes
Tofu (most recipes call for firm)
Canned chickpeas, red kidney beans, white beans, black beans
Steamed or dried lentils
Dried beans if you can get good quality   (*see next page*)

Nuts and Seeds
Raw unsalted walnuts, cashews
Pumpkin, Sunflower, unshelled Hemp seeds
Peanuts
Trail Mix
Nut butter: natural if oil-free

Oils
Olive oil
Grape seed oil
Linseed oil
Toasted sesame seed oil, for stir-fry dishes

Seasonings
Spices (oregano, thyme, rosemary, turmeric/curcuma, cinnamon, vanilla-paste)
Soy sauce (Kikkoman is sugar-free)
Dijon Mustard (sugar free)
Apple Cider vinegar
Vegan mayonnaise (or see recipe here, to make your own with raw cashews)
Hot sauce – if using

Sweetener
Stevia, in liquid form

Other
Pickles (with no sugar added)
Tomato paste
Vegetable broth (fat-free)
Dried fruit – if using (if watching your weight, fresh fruit is a better choice).

NUTRITION and FASTING PRINCIPLES OF HEALTHY*FAST*

Denise Canellos, MS, CNS

Fasting can be incredibly healthy, and provide physical blessings to go along with the spiritual blessings of Lent. When done in a healthy way, fasting can significantly lower our blood cholesterol, blood sugar, and blood pressure, and boost our immune-system. Some of us will even lose some weight during the fast, which can be healthy as well.

Grains

Many problems with fasting come when we replace animal products with refined grains. So much pasta, bread, and white rice! We need so much of these foods to feel full, and they digest very quickly. Choosing whole grain options (e.g., quinoa, buckwheat, whole grain farro, oats) is the way to go. Whole grains are full of fiber, which means they fill us up without filling us out. Whole grains also provide more vitamins and minerals. This means brown rice, whole wheat bread/crackers, and whole grains as side dishes. Pasta from whole grains or bean flours are healthy options too, and the new ones taste like regular pasta - even picky kids can't tell the difference.

Oils

Some of us fast from oil, limit our oil (if we have weight-loss goals), and others do not. In any event, whenever we choose oil it should be a healthy one. Olive, grape seed, sunflower, peanut, and canola oils are all healthy choices for cooking (but olive oil should not be used at very high temperatures). Sesame, linseed and nut oils are fantastic for finishing dishes, but are too delicate for high-heat cooking. Avoid margarine, especially those with trans fat or hydrogenated oils. They are sources of trans-fatty-acids which are harmful to our heart and cardiovascular system. Coconut oil is fine in moderation, but it is high in saturated fats and is not as healthy as the oils that are fluid at room temperature. Deep fat frying is not a healthy option and should be avoided most of the time. Even fried shrimp and fish are special occasion foods. If it is fried with a crunchy coating, it is not the healthiest choice. Foods sautéed in a shallow pan in just a little oil, or if you're fasting oil-free, in water-and-vinegar or oil-free vegetable broth, are much better options Healthy*Fast*ers with weight-loss goals should try limiting their daily intake of added oil to 1-2 Tbs.

Proteins

We often wonder how we will get enough protein when fasting. The truth is protein is in just about every food we eat, and it is rare to be deficient in protein when eating enough calories. Good plant-based protein sources include:

Legumes or beans of all types
Nuts and seeds
Soy products like tofu, tempeh, edamame, soy milk, and soy yogurt
Whole grains such as quinoa, oats, buckwheat, and whole grain farro.

Sugar

The less added sugar we eat, the healthier we are. An occasional vegan treat during Lent is fine, and even helpful if it enables us to keep the fast. Adding sugar to our foods to replace the richness of meat or dairy is a fast-track to weight-gain and diabetes. Our taste buds adjustt to a lower-sugar diet quickly; by the end of Lent you may find many pastries and desserts you used to like now taste overwhelmingly sweet. A note about soda and other sugary beverages - they are not your friends. Switching to water and unsweetened or lightly sweetened tea/coffee will pay off in better health for the rest of your life. If you must sweeten (coffee, a smoothie, etc.), use Stevia (it comes also in liquid-form).

Portions: How much & How often?

Some of the higher-calorie menu plan items have a suggested serving size range, for the average-size adult. This is for those who want to use Lent to achieve some of their weight-loss goals, or at least avoid gaining weight during Lent. The weight-conscious should limit avocados to ½ of an average-size fruit a day; nuts to 1-2 handfuls a day; and limit their daily intake of added oil(s) to 1-2 Tbs a day. Another Healthy*Fast* tip for weight-maintenance is to limit your eating to a 12-hour "window" during the day (for example, have your breakfast at 7 am, and your dinner at 7 pm), and do not eat before or after that window. If weight is not a concern of yours, ignore the serving-size suggestions and eat until you are satisfied. We should not gorge ourselves during Lent, and certainly not lose weight if we are already thin. But one should not get too hungry throughout the work-day to avoid overeating at meal-times; hence a healthy, moderate snack in mid-morning and mid-afternoon (some fruit, nuts, or vegetable-sticks with hummus or tofu-dip, etc.) is suggested in the Healthy*Fast* day. Fruits and vegetables (except white potatoes) are unlimited; the only suggested portion sizes for fruits and vegetables are minimums to get the necessary nutrients in your diet. Indulge in these healthy foods as needed.

Midweek & Weekend "Treats"

Adding some variety to what may feel like a monotony of the fasting diet, the Healthy*Fast* program suggests including "treats" in the middle of one's week (on Wednesdays) and every Saturday and Sunday. Just as the liturgical structure of Orthodox Lent provides the spiritual "treat" of the Liturgy of the Presanctified Gifts on Wednesdays (and Fridays), and the celebration of the Divine Liturgy every Saturday and Sunday (along with the mitigation of fasting, allowing oil & wine on weekends), Healthy*Fast* suggests including in the middle of the week and on weekends some food that one does not have every day, but to which one may look forward, as a sort of "reward" for staying with the sttricter fasting-schedule in between. These "treats" include certain snacks (a fruit-smoothie, popcorn, vegan dessert) and meals (with shellfish, a vegan meat or cheese).

NOTE: You may find it helpful also to integrate a small *daily* "treat" into your fasting-journey, like a small Starbuck's extra-dry cappucino with non-dairy milk (perhaps on your way back from church or from your daily walk), if this makes your fasting-routine more sustainable.

Simple vs. Complicated

Some people prefer a simple way of eating/cooking during Lent, without consulting a recipe, finding it easier to stick to a fasting-program by eating more or less the same thing every day. For these people, the Healthy*Fast* meal-plans include simple options for every meal and snack time. But others may appreciate variety and new ideas/recipes throughout the fast, either for themselves or for their family for which they cook. For these Healthy*Fast*ers there are some less-simple options in the meal-plans, and we will be providing additional Lenten recipes throughout Lent, on a weekly basis.

Plant-based "meats"

There are a lot of plant-based meat replacements on the market now, and some of them are pretty tasty. They can be included in a Lenten diet, but should be included only a couple of times per week (e.g., as your Midweek and/or Weekend Treat). Eating our same meals, just subbing plant-based meat alternatives for real meat, doesn't really accomplish what we need during Lent, and doesn't make us any healthier. So have some vegan "meatballs" or a "burger" when the craving hits, (or better, for your Midweek/Weekend Treat), while most of the time focusing your meals around vegetable and fruits, legumes, and whole grains.

Dairy

For many of us dairy foods are our main source of calcium. Most plant-based milk alternatives are fortified with calcium, so you can get this important mineral from soy, almond, oat, and pea-protein based milks and yogurts. Cheese alternatives made from nuts can also be healthy options.

Vitamins & Other Supplements

Healthy*Fast*ers may want to take a B12 supplement if they are fasting the entire time. It is the one nutrient that is not included in a vegan diet. Other supplements particularly important during the Covid-pandemic, like Vitamin D, if one is deficient in them, should be taken as needed, in consultation with a physician (on the basis of your blood-analysis).

Exercise

During Lent, with its rigorous church-services (with great prostrations), a brisk, uninterrupted walk of just 20-30 minutes in the fresh air is recommended. Before and after Lent, more daily exercise is recommended. That is to say, instead of the Lenten 20-30 minute daily brisk walk, outside of Lent treat yourself to a 40 min-1 hour daily walk in the sunshine (or rain)!

Summary:

Choose whole grains instead of refined grains most of the time. We will get plenty of protein from legumes, nuts, seeds, and soy products. Avoid added sugar most of the time. A dessert once in a while is fine. Reasonable portion sizes will help you avoid any weight gain. Eat as many non-starchy vegetables and fruits as you like. Plant based meat substitutes are fine 1-2 times a week. Plant-based dairy substitutes can be healthy and nutritious. Exercise outdoors is important, both during and outside the fasting-season.

Daily Reflections

for
Every Day of Lent, and Some Days of the Pre- and Post-Lenten Season

Sr. Vassa Larin

Pre-Lent Preparation:
SUNDAY OF THE PUBLICAN & PHARISEE (3 Weeks Before Lent)

KEEPING PRAYER SIMPLE

"He also told this parable to some who trusted in themselves that they were righteous and despised others: 'Two men went up into the temple to pray, one a Pharisee and the other a tax collector. The Pharisee stood and prayed thus with/by himself (πρὸς ἑαυτὸν), 'God, I thank thee that I am not like other men, extortioners, unjust, adulterers, or even like this tax collector. I fast twice a week, I give tithes of all that I get.' But the tax collector, standing far off, would not even lift up his eyes to heaven, but beat his breast, saying, 'God, be merciful to me a sinner!' I tell you, this man went down to his house justified rather than the other; for every one who exalts himself will be humbled, but he who humbles himself will be exalted.'" (Lk 18: 9-14)

The Pharisee is very much "with" or "by" himself, in his prayer. Because it is not God, but his own, human vision of himself and others, that is the focus of his prayer. He has more to say about himself and others than he does about God. The tax collector, on the other hand, simplifies his own vision of human matters, limiting it to "me, a sinner." He has "nothing" to offer God, so he focuses, instead, on God's mercy.

Let me do likewise, and not hesitate to approach God in all honesty, with my "nothing." Let me surrender to Him all judgment over myself and others, keeping my focus simple, on His mercy. As I begin to prepare for Lent, let me give up on my own "something(s)," – like the self-justification that ultimately blocks me from true communion with God and others. Today I choose to keep things simple, and say, "God," I don't know about the rest of it; just "be merciful to me a sinner!"

Meal-Plan (E): *No Fasting Day*
Note: The entire week following this Sunday is fast-free, even on Wednesday and Friday.

MONDAY OF THE PUBLICAN & PHARISEE

GIVE, AND IT WILL BE GIVEN TO YOU

"Judge not, and you will not be judged; condemn not, and you will not be condemned; forgive, and you will be forgiven; give, and it will be given to you; good measure, pressed down, shaken together, running over, will be put into your lap. For the measure you give will be the measure you get back." (Lk 6: 37-38)

…But I can't give what I haven't first received, from God. When I allow the "good" of God into my heart (like forgiveness, mercy, gratitude, humility, and so on), and then pass it on to others, I find it comes back to me. When I'm embracing gratitude, patience, humility, compassion, and perceiving the world in God's light, I find that this light is reflected back onto me, as people, things and places seem friendlier, warmer, and even quite wonderful. On the other hand, when I disconnect with God's grace, and carry around ingratitude, resentments, self-centered expectations and demands (of myself and/or others), etc., then everything and everyone suddenly doesn't "measure up." And I waste time being like an open wound, sensitive to every little thing.

Let me re-connect with God this morning, surrendering to Him all the empty space in my heart. I accept His mercy this morning, His love and generosity, toward me and others, that I may carry it with me, and pass it on, throughout my day. "Our Father, Who art in heaven!" I say to God as I begin this Monday. "Thy will be done" with all of us today, Lord, as You see fit.

Meal-Plan (E): *No Fasting Day*
*Note: This entire week is fast-free, even on Wednesday and Friday.

> For more on this phase of our pre-Lent preparation, tune in weekdays to the "Morning Coffee" audio-podcast at **patreon.com/sistervassa**. Leave a comment and say hello to fellow Healthy*Fast*ers, and start all your Healthy*Fast* weekdays with us, because fasting is teamwork!

TUESDAY OF THE PUBLICAN & PHARISEE

PATIENCE IN LOCKDOWN

"But take heed to yourselves/watch yourselves (βλέπετε…ἑαυτούς); for they will deliver you up to councils; and you will be beaten in synagogues; and you will stand before governors and kings for my sake, to bear testimony before them. And the gospel must first be preached to all nations. And when they bring you to trial and deliver you up, do not be anxious beforehand what you are to say; but say whatever is given you in that hour, for it is not you who speak, but the Holy Spirit. And brother will deliver up brother to death, and the father his child, and children will rise against parents and have them put to death; and you will be hated by all for my name's sake. But he who has patience (ὑπομείνας) to the end will be saved." (Mk 13: 9-13)

I need to "take heed to," or "watch" my "self," that I have "patience" or "hypo-mone" in Greek, – which means, literally, a "remaining behind," – whenever "they" bring me "to trial" on my cross-carrying journey. Who are "they"? It's whoever and whatever, either within or outside me, that pulls me away from being the "self" Christ calls me to be, according to my "vocation."

Let me "remain behind," in patience, and let the Holy Spirit "speak" in my home this Tuesday, so I don't waste time on "other" voices calling me to be elsewhere; to be restless at this time of Covid-lockdowns. These "calls" may lead me to waste an opportunity to grow, and to get my own "house" in order. Let me replace fear with faith today, and open up to God's grace in some heartfelt prayer, that I may let Him take the lead, and myself follow, from "behind," in patience. "Lead us not into temptation," Lord, "and deliver us from the evil one," that we take this pre-Lenten time to get more focused on You.

Meal-Plan (E): *No Fasting Day*
*Note: This entire week is fast-free, even on Wednesday and Friday.

WEDNESDAY OF THE PUBLICAN & PHARISEE

LET YOUR LIGHT SHINE

"You are the light of the world. A city set on a hill cannot be hid. Nor do men light a lamp and put it under a bushel, but on a stand, and it gives light to all in the house. Let your light so shine before men, that they may see your good works and give glory to your Father who is in heaven." (Mt 5: 14-16)

This passage is read on the feasts of certain great saints, who "let" the "light of the world," Christ (Jn 8: 12), "so shine" through them, that it lit up the lives of all who encountered them.

When I choose to "let" Christ light up my life, connecting with Him in my heart, I can also be of service to others, shining love onto hatred, forgiveness onto wrong, harmony onto discord, hope onto despair, faith onto doubt, and so on. Conversely I can choose to wallow in my own darkness, like self-reliance, self-pity, and self-centered fears, which ultimately exacerbate the darkness of others around me. Lord, may Your light shine in our darkness today, by the prayers of all Your saints, as we walk toward the upcoming Lenten season.

Meal-Plan (E): *No Fasting Day*
*Note: This entire week is fast-free, even on Wednesday and Friday.

THURSDAY OF THE PUBLICAN & PHARISEE

IMAGINE THERE'S NO HEAVEN

"Heaven and earth will pass away, but my words will not pass away." (Mk 13: 31)

Which "heaven" will "pass away"? The sky we see above us. It's not the "no heaven" that John Lennon called us to "imagine," with "above us, only sky," no. In fact this sky, this earth, along with the words of John Lennon, will pass away. *"But according to his* (the Lord's) *promise,"* as St. Peter explains, *"we wait for new heavens and a new earth in which righteousness dwells."* (2 Pet 3: 13) All this will pass, to be fully made over, and made "new" by our One Creator, by His life-creating Word.

Let me also be made new this morning, once again, by the ever-life-creating words of our Lord, which will not pass away. I need not be dragged down by merely-human words and imaginings, either those in my head or those coming at me throughout my day. I can take a bit of time for some prayerful reading, and be lifted up, in gratitude, into Truth and Light and Life. *"I am the light of the world,"* the Lord says to me today. *"Whoever follows me will not walk in darkness, but will have the light of life."* (Jn 8: 12) Glory be to Him.

Meal-Plan (E): *No Fasting Day*
Note: *This entire week is fast-free, even on Wednesday and Friday.*

CONFESSING TO "SIN"

"If we say we have no sin (ὅτι ἁμαρτίαν οὐκ ἔχομεν), we deceive ourselves, and the truth is not in us. If we confess our sins, he is faithful and just, and will forgive our sins and cleanse us from all unrighteousness." (1 Jn 1: 8-9)

Is "sin" all that hard to admit, before a "faithful and just" God? No, not really. Because He can and "will," indeed, "forgive" and "cleanse" me. It's much more complicated, I'd say, to burden myself with self-justification, as did the Pharisee in the parable we contemplate this week. It takes altogether more "work" and more unnecessary words.

To say that I have no "sin" (ἁμαρτία in Greek, meaning, "to miss the mark") means to be in burdensome denial, about the "truth" of myself and others. Because, time and again, I do miss "the mark," which is God's specific call to me, or my "vocation," to do what I am supposed to be doing, in the here and now. If I don't have an honest, humble vision of how I do not hit that "mark," at times, of His way for me, I will also have a distorted, not-compassionate vision of the "truth" about other people around me.

Today let me not fear honesty, before my merciful and just God, and take a few minutes for self-examination. Let me unburden myself from any masks I feel compelled to wear, (I don't mean the ones that are Covid-related, but) before human opinion, and re-connect with God in honest, heartfelt prayer, as I am. Lord, let me have the joy and peace of knowing my "sin" as You know it, in Your undying love, justice and mercy. Amen!

Meal-Plan (E): *No Fasting Day*
*Note: *This entire week is fast-free, even on Wednesday and Friday.*

SATURDAY OF THE PUBLICAN & PHARISEE

DOING OUR JOBS WITH LOVE

"One of the Pharisees asked him to eat with him, and he went into the Pharisee's house, and took his place at table. And behold, a woman of the city, who was a sinner, when she learned that he was at table in the Pharisee's house, brought an alabaster flask of ointment, and standing behind him at his feet, weeping, she began to wet his feet with her tears, and wiped them with the hair of her head, and kissed his feet, and anointed them with the ointment. Now when the Pharisee who had invited him saw it, he said to himself, 'If this man were a prophet, he would have known who and what sort of woman this is who is touching him, for she is a sinner.' And Jesus answering said to him, 'Simon, I have something to say to you.' And he answered, 'What is it, Teacher?' 'A certain creditor had two debtors; one owed five hundred denarii, and the other fifty. When they could not pay, he forgave them both. Now which of them will love him more?' Simon answered, 'The one, I suppose, to whom he forgave more.' And he said to him, 'You have judged rightly.' Then turning toward the woman he said to Simon, 'Do you see this woman? I entered your house, you gave me no water for my feet, but she has wet my feet with her tears and wiped them with her hair. You gave me no kiss, but from the time I came in she has not ceased to kiss my feet. You did not anoint my head with oil, but she has anointed my feet with ointment. Therefore I tell you, her sins, which are many, are forgiven, for she loved much; but he who is forgiven little, loves little.'" (Lk 7: 36-47)

Simon the Pharisee went down in history as a terrible host. He got to receive the God-Man in his house, and yet failed to offer Him the basic hospitality, customary at that time. Simon was too busy judging his Guest ("If this man were a prophet…") to notice the blunders in his own "job-performance," as host, or to recognize Who it was he was hosting. He entirely missed the opportunity to encounter God on this occasion, because he put so "little love" into it.

Today, whatever job I am called to do for or with other people, whether professionally or socially, let me approach my vocation with a loving heart, and with mindfulness of my own responsibilities. Love opens my eyes to God's presence and wisdom in my life and work, whereas self-centered expectations tend to blind me to His goodness and make me less effective for Him, myself, and others. *"I will love you, O Lord, my strength; the Lord is my foundation, my refuge, and my deliverer."* (Ps 17: 2-3a).

Meal-Plan (E): *No Fasting Day*

SATURDAY OF THE PUBLICAN & PHARISEE

COMING TO MYSELF

"And he said, 'There was a man who had two sons; and the younger of them said to his father, 'Father, give me the share of property that falls to me.' And he divided his living between them. Not many days later, the younger son gathered all he had and took his journey into a far country, and there he squandered his property in loose living. And when he had spent everything, a great famine arose in that country, and he began to be in want. So he went and joined himself to one of the citizens of that country, who sent him into his fields to feed swine. And he would gladly have fed on the pods that the swine ate; and no one gave him anything. But when he came to himself (εἰς ἑαυτὸν δὲ ἐλθὼν) *he said, 'How many of my father's hired servants have bread enough and to spare, but I perish here with hunger! I will arise and go to my father, and I will say to him, 'Father, I have sinned against heaven and before you; I am no longer worthy to be called your son; treat me as one of your hired servants.' And he arose and came to his father. But while he was yet at a distance, his father saw him and had compassion, and ran and embraced him and kissed him…"* (Lk 15: 11-20)

The prodigal son had first to come "to himself," before he could come "home" to his family. Earlier, he had lost touch with his "self," while he was living recklessly. He had lost touch with the self God called him to be, according to his "vocation." While he was being tossed to and fro by "other" calls, not God's, the prodigal son had no true identity, and lived in some "distant country" that was not his place.

As we continue to prepare for Lent, the season of renewal, let me not be reluctant to come to my "self," and take a look at any motivations or ambitions that may be tossing me to and fro, causing me to "miss the mark" to which God calls me. And let me not fear coming "home," to where I always have a home, and am accepted as my "self," warts and all, in God's embrace. Our Father, Who art in heaven, forgive us our debts, as we forgive our debtors. Amen!

Meal-Plan (E): *No Fasting Day*
Note: *This upcoming Meatfare Week is the final week that we eat meat, before Pascha.*

MONDAY OF MEATFARE WEEK

MARTYRDOM & BEARING WITNESS

"The maid who kept the door said to Peter, 'Are not you also one of this man's disciples?' He said, 'I am not.'" (Jn 18:18)

Peter is the same man who, earlier in this very chapter of the Gospel according to John, drew a sword when our Lord was arrested in Gethsemane, and in a vain attempt to "stand up" for His Master, cut off the right ear of the high priest's slave (Jn 18: 10). But nobody asked or "called" Peter to do that. Yet a bit later, as we see above, when he is truly "called" to stand up and be counted as one of the Lord's disciples in a less dramatic way, – to respond truthfully to a maid's simple question, – he fails to do so.

So the call to being a "martyr" or "witness" to the Lord does not always come wrapped in heroism and extraodinary chivalry. It might come to me in my everyday, undramatic circumstances, when I am trying to "blend in" or "belong" in ways that I should not. Lord, grant me the courage to be the true "me" I am in You, regardless of the circumstances. Amen!

Meal-Plan (E): *No Fasting Day*
*Note: This Meatfare week is the final week that we eat meat, before Pascha.

For more on this phase of our pre-Lent preparation, tune in weekdays to the "Morning Coffee" audio-podcast at **patreon.com/sistervassa**. Leave a comment and say hello to fellow Healthy*Fast*ers, and start all your Healthy*Fast* weekdays with us, because fasting is teamwork!

TUESDAY OF MEATFARE WEEK

WATCH AND PRAY

"And they went to a place which was called Gethsemane; and he said to his disciples, 'Sit here, while I pray.' And he took with him Peter and James and John, and began to be greatly distressed and troubled. And he said to them, 'My soul is very sorrowful, even to death; remain here, and watch.' And going a little farther, he fell on the ground and prayed that, if it were possible, the hour might pass from him. And he said, 'Abba, Father, all things are possible to you; remove this cup from me; yet not what I will, but what you will.' And he came and found them sleeping, and he said to Peter, 'Simon, are you asleep? Could you not watch one hour? Watch and pray that you may not enter into temptation; the spirit indeed is willing, but the flesh is weak.' And again he went away and prayed, saying the same words." (Mk 14: 32-39)

The God Man does two things, when His soul is "very sorrowful, even unto death": 1. He shares this with His closest friends, and 2. He prays, physically falling on the ground, and surrendering the anguish over His "cup" to the will of the Father.

Emotional anguish, like great sorrow and fear, also affect "the flesh," making heavy or bogging down the body into inactivity, which easily leads to more insecurity and fear. However, while "the flesh is weak," as the Lord notes here, "the spirit indeed is willing." And in us and with us, indeed, the Holy Spirit is "willing" to continue on the cross-carrying, life-affirming journey, even when it gets to be too much for "the flesh." So let me remember Him, the Giver of Life, when my soul is "very sorrowful, even unto death." Let me reach out, as best I can, to Another and also others around me, in humble honesty, surrendering my weakness to God's life-creating will. Let me "fall down" before Him, rather than "fall down" into inactivity, when I am weak. Let me "watch" or remain "awake" to the Spirit in these pre-Lenten weeks, as I pick up His tools of healthy-fasting, prayer, and the fellowship of our common, upcoming Lenten journey.

Meal-Plan (E): *No Fasting Day*
Note:** **This Meatfare week is the final week that we eat meat, before Pascha.

WEDNESDAY OF MEATFARE WEEK

ON SEX & POWER

"The scribes and the Pharisees brought a woman who had been caught in adultery, and placing her in the midst they said to him, 'Teacher, this woman has been caught in the act of adultery. Now in the law Moses commanded us to stone such women (τὰς τοιαύτας). What do you say about her?' This they said to test him, that they might have some charge to bring against him. Jesus bent down and wrote with his finger on the ground. And as they continued to ask him, he stood up and said to them, 'Let him who is without sin among you be the first to throw a stone at her.' And once more he bent down and wrote with his finger on the ground. But when they heard it, they went away, one by one, beginning with the eldest, and Jesus was left alone with the woman standing before him. Jesus looked up and said to her, 'Woman, where are they? Has no one condemned you?' She said, 'No one, Lord.' And Jesus said, 'Neither do I condemn you; go, and do not sin again.'" (Jn 8: 3-11)

There's a touch of male-chauvinism in the claim of the scribes and Pharisees, that the Law commanded the stoning of "such women." Because the Law, actually, spoke of the death of both the man and the woman involved in adultery (Lev 20: 10; Deut 22: 22-24). But we see no evidence here of any man being brought to justice. We only see men, the scribes and Pharisees, dragging a woman, whom they had "caught," by the power they wielded, into the "midst" of public humiliation.

As some commentators have hypothesized, Jesus perhaps wrote with His finger some of the sins (sexual ones), of which the scribes and Pharisees were themselves guilty. Be that as it may, the sin of these men was primarily about power, while the sin of the woman was primarily about sex. Even if it's hard to disentangle the two, in many confrontations between males and females (like the ones in our day, involving sexual harassment / misconduct), our Lord exonerates the woman, entirely power-less in the situation as it was presented to Jesus, by the power-ful men who sought her death before Him. Because the abuse/misstep of their power, in His eyes, was apparently more insidious, and more important to check, than the abuse/misstep of sex, in her situation. The latter, (sex), was a gift common to everyone, both to this woman and her accusers, while the former, (power), was one endowed to a select few, like these men with religious authority. So their responsibility and accountability was graver. But our Lord also lets them off the hook rather easily, as far as I can see, letting them walk away, because they didn't know any better as men of their time.

Lord, have mercy on all of us, in matters of sex and power, and in matters where both intertwine. Help us wield all Your gifts according to Your will and love for us, in love and compassion for one another. Amen!

Meal Plan (A): ***Strict Fast Day with No Oil***
TIP: This fast-day is a good opportunity to "practice" for upcoming Lent! Try it "with oil," according to Meal Plan **(B)**, *if you always fast with oil.*

THURSDAY OF MEATFARE WEEK

CHOOSING CHRIST OVER BARABBAS

"Now at the feast he used to release for them one prisoner for whom they asked. And among the rebels in prison, who had committed murder in the insurrection, there was a man called Barabbas. And the crowd came up and began to ask Pilate to do as he was wont to do for them. And he answered them, 'Do you want me to release for you the King of the Jews?' For he perceived that it was out of envy that the chief priests had delivered him up. But the chief priests stirred up the crowd to have him release for them Barabbas instead. And Pilate again said to them, 'Then what shall I do with the man whom you call the King of the Jews?' And they cried out again, 'Crucify him.' And Pilate said to them, 'Why, what evil has he done?' But they shouted all the more, 'Crucify him.' So Pilate, wishing to satisfy the crowd, released for them Barabbas; and having scourged Jesus, he delivered him to be crucified." (Mk 15: 6-15)

So the crowd chooses Barabbas, a known murderer, over Jesus, known recently to have raised one Lazarus from the dead. Our Lord was also known as a healer, and as a preacher of repentance, forgiveness, true love, life, and freedom in the Spirit. But as such, He has become unbearable for the people He loves. They prefer to have a murderer, Barabbas, released into their midst, rather than continue to be challenged by divine love.

God's true love is hard to endure, when my heart is tied up by other, self-centered "loves" and their resulting fears. They delude me into cherishing going around in their circles, which seem to "protect" me from the painstaking process of growth in true love. But Christ calls me daily to a new freedom in Him, guiding me, when I am willing to listen, through the process of salvation from this "bondage of self." This process takes some work, like a bit of prayer and self-examination on a daily basis. But it's not burdensome or dark, – not like having a Barabbas roaming free in my neighborhood. Today let me allow Christ into my "neighborhood," and re-connect with Him in some heartfelt prayer. "For my yoke is easy," He reassures me ahead of Lent, "and my burden is light." (Mt 11: 30)

Meal-Plan (E): *No Fasting Day*
*Note: This Meatfare week is the final week that we eat meat, before Pascha.

FRIDAY OF MEATFARE WEEK

CHRIST AND CLOTHING

"And they brought him to the place called Golgotha (which means the place of a skull). And they offered him wine mingled with myrrh; but he did not take it. And they crucified him, and divided his garments among them, casting lots for them, to decide what each should take." (Mk 15: 22-24)

On that Friday two millennia ago, each of the four soldiers who crucified our Lord "won" a piece of His garments for himself. And Christ let them "win" in this way, as He knew they would, as was revealed in an ancient prophecy found in Psalm 21/22: *"They have divided my garments amongst themselves, and for my clothing have they cast lots."* (Ps 21/22: 18) So these soldiers got to be clothed in Christ's garments, and He let them do that.

Why? So that we, who choose to surrender to Him, rather than "win" over Him, can be "clothed" not merely in garments but in Him, in His very Body: *"For as many of you as have been baptized into Christ have put on Christ."* (Gal 3: 27) In Baptism, God no longer clothes us (only) in "garments of skin," as He lovingly does for us in our fallen state (Gen 3:21), ever since we chose to burden ourselves with the painful self-awareness that comes from eating of "the tree of knowledge of good and evil." Those garments are just a "band-aid" to help us deal with that self-awareness, while we are still works-in-progress on our cross-carrying journeys. But our new "clothing" is not in the old Adam but in Christ, Who is clothed in "majesty" or "beauty" (εὐπρέπειαν ἐνεδύσατο, в лЕпоту облечеся, Ps 92/93: 1).

Today let me let Christ clothe me His way, and make me beautiful again, with Himself. Let me embrace Him, as He embraces me and all of us, with His hands outstretched on the Cross. *"Remember me, Lord, when You come into Your kingdom!"* (Lk 23: 42)

Meal Plan (A): ***Strict Fast Day with No Oil***
*TIP: This fast-day is a good opportunity to "practice" for upcoming Lent! Try it "with oil," according to Meal Plan (B), if you always fast with oil.

MEMORIAL SATURDAY OF MEATFARE WEEK

KILL YOUR DARLINGS

"Wretched daughter of Babylon! ...Blessed shall he be who shall seize and dash your infants against the rock." (Ps 136/137: 8a, 9, Septuagint-translation)

In his little book "On Writing," the great novelist Stephen King uses a similar image to advise the inexperienced writer about the painful editing process: "Kill your darlings," he says. He means that the writer should not hesitate to cross out (or delete) all unnecessary details, no matter how much he or she loves them.

The Psalm is also talking about "infants" that I tend to love, within myself. They are sinful thoughts, at first small and weak, of various types of wishful thinking, lustful thinking, fearful thinking, resentful thinking, and so on. These "infants" need to be "dashed" against the "rock," – my Rock and my Hope, Jesus Christ. May I get rid of any creepy "infants" today and let Him take care of them, before they grow and take over my house. "Lord Jesus Christ, Son of God," be my Rock this season, as we approach the liberating house-cleaning that is Lent. Amen.

Meal-Plan (E): *No Fasting Day*
Note: Tomorrow is the last day that we eat meat, before Pascha.

MEATFARE SUNDAY (OF THE LAST JUDGMENT, 1 WEEK BEFORE LENT)

GOD'S JUDGMENT & OURS

"...Then he will say to those at his left hand, 'You that are accursed, depart from me into the eternal fire prepared for the devil and his angels; for I was hungry and you gave me no food, I was thirsty and you gave me nothing to drink, I was a stranger and you did not welcome me, naked and you did not give me clothing, sick and in prison and you did not visit me.' Then they also will answer, 'Lord, when was it that we saw you hungry or thirsty or a stranger or naked or sick or in prison, and did not take care of you?' Then he will answer them, 'Truly I tell you, just as you did not do it to one of the least of these, you did not do it to me.' And these will go away into eternal punishment, but the righteous into eternal life." (Mt 25: 41-46)

Here are some thoughts for anyone who, like me, has failed to feed the hungry, give drink to the thirsty, offer welcome to the stranger, clothe the naked, and visit the sick and imprisoned. How could I justify myself before God, were I to pass away today? I couldn't, and I shouldn't. If I've got nothing before God, I appeal to Him as did the tax-collector, with his nothing, *"God, have mercy on me, the sinner!"* Or at least as did the prodigal son to his father, with no sense of entitlement: *"I am no longer worthy to be called your son. Treat me as one of your hired servants!"*

And here's another "get-out-of-jail-free card" God offers to me: Forgive others, and you will be forgiven. Do not judge others, and you will not be judged. So let me let things go today, even long-standing resentments and grudges, because God calls me to do for others what I want Him to do for me, – to forgive a whole lot of "debt" just like that, in exchange for nothing.

"Forgive us our debts, as we forgive our debtors," Lord, and help us let go of the pointlessness of self-justification and merely-human judgment. For Thine is the kingdom, the power, the glory, and, indeed, the judgment. Amen!

Meal-Plan (E): *No Fasting Day*
*Note: Today is the last day that we eat meat, before Pascha. In the upcoming Cheesefare week, dairy-products and fish are allowed (also on Wednesday and Friday), but no meat or poultry.

MONDAY OF CHEESEFARE WEEK

THE LORD'S ANONYMOUS HELPERS

"When he drew near to Bethphage and Bethany, at the mount that is called Olivet, he sent two of the disciples, saying, 'Go into the village opposite, where on entering you will find a colt tied, on which no one has ever yet sat; untie it and bring it here. If any one asks you, Why are you untying it? you shall say this, The Lord has need of it.' So those who were sent went away and found it as he had told them. And as they were untying the colt, its owners said to them, 'Why are you untying the colt?' And they said, 'The Lord has need of it.' And they brought it to Jesus, and throwing their garments on the colt they set Jesus upon it." (Lk 19: 29-35)

We see these nameless followers of the Lord in the Gospel-narratives, like the owners of this colt, who are ready to give it up, simply because they learn that "the Lord has need of it." Three chapters later in this same Gospel, another anonymous benefactor provides a "guest room" for the Lord, in which He has requested to "eat the Passover" with His disciples, when Peter and John show up to this man's house with that request (Lk 22: 7-13).

I don't know anything about these people, not even their names. They made no known contribution to spreading the "word" as did the Apostles, or other famous saints. And yet their small, material donation (of a colt, and of a room) played a vital role in Salvation History. Thank You, Lord, both for the named and the unnamed heroes of our Tradition, who have served You and us, to Your greater glory in our world. And let me not neglect to thank You today, for those in my world whose names I don't know, but who have done me small kindnesses, – like the bus-driver who returned my wallet when I had lost it in his bus; or like the stranger who let me use his phone at the airport, when my phone ran out of charge. And thank You for those who pray for me, while I don't even know them. *"Bless the Lord, all His works, in all places of His dominion. Bless the Lord, O my soul!"*

Meal Plan (D): *Cheesefare/Maslenitsa Week – no meat or poultry, but dairy-products and fish allowed this entire week, including Wednesday and Friday*

For more on this phase of our pre-Lent preparation, tune in weekdays to the "Morning Coffee" audio-podcast at **patreon.com/sistervassa**. Leave a comment and say hello to fellow Healthy*Fast*ers, and start all your Healthy*Fast* weekdays with us, because fasting is teamwork!

TUESDAY OF CHEESEFARE WEEK

"PROCESSING" THE NEWS, IN LIGHT OF THE CROSS

"Now the men who were holding Jesus mocked him and beat him; they also blindfolded him and asked him, 'Prophesy! Who is it that struck you?' And they spoke many other words against him, reviling him." (Lk 22: 63-65)

Does it do us any good, to know the heartbreaking details of certain egregious crimes, like the ones described above? They blindfolded Him, beat Him, mocked Him, and apparently they enjoyed it. You can't "un-know" that; it stays with you, like stories and images that pop up in the news, of various forms of human cruelty, shamelessness, vandalism, etc. How can I "process" this information, that I might carry from it wisdom, rather than cynicism, about our humanity in general?

I can "process" it in the light of the dark story quoted above, of God's only-begotten Son subjecting Himself to that kind of human darkness, in His kind of humanity. He takes it all on and absorbs it, in His Self-offering. He walks through it even unto death and downwards into our hell, forgives it and overcomes it in His new life, emerging from our hell and our tomb in His glorious resurrection. In the com-passionate (co-suffering) cross of our Lord Jesus Christ, Who has suffered with the victimized in this world, and allowed Himself to be crucified in the midst of two criminals, one can discern light, both for the victims and the criminals. Let me choose communion with Him today, in some heartfelt prayer, and participate in His kind of humanity, the divinized kind that self-offers in the midst of criminals. Remember us all, Lord, the criminals and the victims, when You come into Your kingdom!

Meal Plan (D): *Cheesefare/Maslenitsa Week – no meat or poultry, but dairy-products and fish allowed this entire week, including Wednesday and Friday*

WEDNESDAY OF CHEESEFARE WEEK

REND YOUR HEARTS NOT YOUR CLOTHING

"Yet even now, says the Lord, return to me with all your heart, with fasting, with weeping, and with mourning; rend your hearts and not your clothing. Return to the Lord, your God, for he is gracious and merciful, slow to anger, and abounding in steadfast love, and relents from punishing." (Joel 2: 12-13)

This is part of our Church's reading for today, Cheesefare Wednesday. Because this week preceding Lent, or Cheesefare Week (Maslenitsa in Russian), is liturgically already preparing us for the season of fasting and "return to the Lord" that is Lent. In fact, today, on Cheesefare Wednesday, the Divine Liturgy is not celebrated, and the Lenten Prayer of St. Ephrem is read throughout the services of the Hours or the Divine Office (with great prostrations), according to the order prescribed by the Typikon for this day, so as to prepare us for the upcoming season of Lent.

Today let me take a bit of time for some pre-Lenten preparations, both spiritual and physical. As I'm called to do in the passage quoted above, I "rend my heart and not my clothing." So I take care of my clothing and other physical needs (as the Lord says elsewhere, "when you fast, anoint your head and wash your face," Mt 6:17), and also begin to stock my pantry with some of the beans, grains, healthy pasta, etc., which I will need for healthy-fasting beginning next Monday. And let me begin to return to the Lord "with all my heart," in heartfelt prayer, "for he is gracious and merciful, slow to anger, and abounding in steadfast love, and relents from punishing," as our Church's reading for today reminds me.

Meal Plan (D): *Cheesefare/Maslenitsa Week – no meat or poultry, but dairy-products and fish allowed this entire week, including Wednesday and Friday*

THURSDAY OF CHEESEFARE WEEK

PLANNING A SUSTAINABLE LENT

"And whoever does not bear his cross and come after me cannot be my disciple. For which of you, intending to build a tower, does not sit down first and count the cost, whether he has enough to finish it—lest, after he has laid the foundation, and is not able to finish, all who see it begin to mock him, saying, 'This man began to build and was not able to finish'? Or what king, going to make war against another king, does not sit down first and consider whether he is able with ten thousand to meet him who comes against him with twenty thousand? Or else, while the other is still a great way off, he sends a delegation and asks conditions of peace. So likewise, whoever of you does not forsake all that he has cannot be My disciple." (Lk 14: 27-33)

"Being a disciple" of our Lord includes bearing the cross of our own limitations by recognizing them, surrendering them to God's will, and following Christ in the way we are given to do, within our circumstances. This means: 1. Not taking on the type of overly-elaborate "building projects" that we can't finish; and 2. Having the humble wisdom to negotiate "conditions of peace" with those adverse circumstances against which we cannot wage all-out war.

Here's what this tells me about planning a fasting and praying rule for Lent. I surrender my self-reliant ideas about my own "will power," and instead "sit down" and consider how I can integrate into the upcoming seven weeks the gentle discipline of Lent. Can I make it to church for some or any weekday Lenten services? How can I in my home and/or work-environment find the time/space for some daily prayer? Do I need to negotiate some "conditions of peace" with loved ones or colleagues who are not fasting, (by saying something like, Hey here's what I'll be doing, and please don't freak out or anything because I am trying to get healthy)? Can I fast oil-free on all weekdays? Or should I fast with oil? Or limit it to 1-2 Tbs daily? Might I integrate little healthy snacks in between my meals, (ca. 3 hours before and after the midday meal) to avoid overeating at mealtimes? Might I include some "treats" here and there, (suggested in the Healthy*Fast* program on Wednesdays and weekends)? Where in my day can I fit in some healthy exercise?

Whatever daily/weekly discipline I decide on, let me remember not to throw the baby out with the bath water, that is to say, to just opt out of any discipline at all. Because I do want to be Your "disciple," Lord, but can't do that without Your gentle "discipline." Grant me the serenity to accept the things I cannot change, the courage to change the things I can, and the wisdom to know the difference!

Meal Plan (D): *Cheesefare/Maslenitsa Week – no meat or poultry, but dairy-products and fish allowed this entire week, including Wednesday and Friday*

FRIDAY OF CHEESEFARE WEEK

"WE WILL GO WITH YOU"

"Thus says the Lord of hosts; The fast of the fourth month, and the fast of the fifth, and the fast of the seventh, and the fast of the tenth, shall be to the house of Judah joy and gladness, and cheerful feasts; therefore love the truth and peace. Thus says the Lord of hosts; It shall yet come to pass, that there shall come people, and the inhabitants of many cities: And the inhabitants of one city shall go to another, saying, Let us go speedily to pray before the Lord, and to seek the Lord of hosts: I will go also. Yea, many people and strong nations shall come to seek the Lord of hosts in Jerusalem, and to pray before the Lord. Thus says the Lord of hosts; In those days ten men from every language of the nations shall grasp the garment of a Jewish man, saying, 'We will go with you: for we have heard that God is with you.'" (Zechariah 8: 19-23)

This is the reading at Vespers today, on Cheesefare-Friday, a day when no Divine Liturgy is celebrated, and our church-services include other Lenten moments, like the Prayer of St. Ephrem with great prostrations. As Lent is just two days away, the prophetic text reminds me that times of fasting are times of "joy and gladness."

It also speaks prophetically of our time, the era of the Church and her beautiful traditions, like Lent, when "many people and strong nations," like ours in both East and West, "shall come to seek the Lord of hosts in Jerusalem." We direct our gaze toward Jerusalem, the Holy City where one Jesus of Nazareth was crucified, buried, and resurrected on the third day, according to the Scriptures, as we begin our Lenten journey toward Great/Holy Week and Pascha. In our day people like us, "from every language of the nations," from all over the world, "grasp the garment of a Jewish man," – the garment of our Lord Jesus Christ that is His Church, saying, "We will go with you; for we have heard that God is with you."

So let me re-direct my gaze toward Jerusalem today, and toward the Cross erected there two millennia ago, as I reach out and "grasp the garment of a Jewish man," Who leads me to renewal, in the life-affirming season of Lent. "We will go with you," Lord, as You lead us on the Lenten journey, re-teaching us to "love the truth and peace." Amen!

Meal Plan (D): *Cheesefare/Maslenitsa Week – no meat or poultry, but dairy-products and fish allowed this entire week, including Wednesday and Friday*
*TIP: You might begin stocking your pantry, if you haven't done so yet, with some of the beans, grains, non-dairy milk & yogurt, etc., which you'll be needing next Monday!

SATURDAY OF CHEESEFARE WEEK (Saturday Before Lent, of All Ascetical Fathers)

THE DOORS OF REPENTANCE

"Open to me the doors/gates (πύλας) of repentance, O Giver of Life: for early in the morning my spirit seeks Your holy temple, bearing a temple of the body all defiled. But in Your compassion cleanse it by Your loving-kindness and mercy." (Byzantine Hymn at Sunday Matins before and during Lent)

This pre-Lenten (and Lenten) hymn reminds me of "doors" that are presently closed. Otherwise I would not be asking for them to be opened. The fact is, I have closed the way leading to change, or "change of mind" ("metanoia" or repentance), having stagnated in certain, habitual patterns that "defile" (from "defouler," to trample down) or "trample down" my growth in God, the Giver of Life. And I need help, when it comes to making a change and opening those "doors" again, leading to change.

So this is an exciting time, this pre-Lenten season, which speaks primarily of change; a change I can enter into, when I pick up the simple tools laid out before me in the prayers, discipline, and atmosphere of Lent. It reminds me of the exciting time when John the Baptist first proclaimed a great change that was coming, as he "prepared the way of the Lord" and *"went into all the region around the Jordan, proclaiming a baptism of repentance for the forgiveness of sins..."* (Lk 3: 3) So let me join in and embrace this season of change; a change I can believe in.

Meal Plan (D): *Cheesefare/Maslenitsa Week – no meat or poultry, but dairy-products and fish allowed*
*TIP: It's time to stock your pantry and fridge, if you haven't done so yet, with some of the beans, grains, non-dairy milk & yogurt, etc., which you'll be needing next Monday!

FORGIVENESS SUNDAY (Adam's Exile from Paradise)

GOD-FOCUSED FASTING

"And whenever you fast, do not look dismal, like the hypocrites, for they disfigure their faces so as to show people (τοῖς ἀνθρώποις) that they are fasting. Truly I tell you, they have received their reward. But when you fast, put oil on your head and wash your face, so that you do not appear as fasting to people (τοῖς ἀνθρώποις), but to your Father who is in secret; and your Father who sees in secret will reward you. Do not store up for yourselves treasures on earth, where moth and rust consume and where thieves break in and steal; but store up for yourselves treasures in heaven, where neither moth nor rust consumes and where thieves do not break in and steal. For where your treasure is, there your heart will be also." (Mt 6: 16-21)

Fasting is good for me, no doubt about it. It is good for me both physically and spiritually. In fact today we fast more readily for physical reasons than for spiritual ones, I think, although both are interconnected and most effectively tackled together.

But in any event, it is bad for my heart to engage in fasting with "people" as my target audience. That is to say, it is disorienting for my heart, because people-pleasing makes me chase the changeable winds of human opinions, tastes, and expectations – including my own.

So let me dispense with "doing it for myself," as I am often advised, and with doing it for the "body image" considered most fashionable by people today. Let me rather have God as my target audience, as I care for my spiritual and physical "house," a treasure He entrusted to me. And let me prepare to fast according to my "vocation," which is comprised of all the various aspects of my life and character, with its strengths and weaknesses, known in their entirety only to God. I ask Him today to build with me this work-in-progress that is me, relying on His wisdom to develop and function properly. Let my heart be in Your hands, O Lord, like a treasure-in-progress in this fasting season. Amen!

Meal Plan (D): *Cheesefare/Maslenitsa Week – Today is the last day dairy-products are allowed until Pascha*
*TIP: This evening you might clear your fridge of dairy-products and other non-Lenten foods, (eat and/or freeze what you can), and see to it that you have what you need for tomorrow.

1st Week of Lent
MONDAY, 1st Week (Clean Monday, Beginning of the Holy and Great 40 Days)

COME, LET US REASON TOGETHER

"Hear, O heaven, and hearken, O earth: for the Lord has spoken, saying, I have begotten and reared up children, but they have rebelled against me. The ox knows his owner, and the ass his master's crib: but Israel does not know me, and the people has not regarded me… Your fasting, and rest from work, your new moons also, and your feasts my soul hates: you have become loathsome to me; I will no more pardon your sins. When you stretch forth your hands, I will turn away my eyes from you: and though you make many supplications, I will not hearken to you; for your hands are full of blood. Wash you, be clean; remove your iniquities from your souls before my eyes; cease from your iniquities; learn to do well; diligently seek judgment, deliver him that is suffering wrong, plead for the orphan, and obtain justice for the widow. And come, let us reason together, saith the Lord: and though your sins be as purple, I will make them white as snow; and though they be as scarlet, I will make them white as wool…" (Is 1: 2-3, 14-18)

This is one of the readings for today, the first day of Lent. And what an unexpected reading it is. God tells us, among other things, "Your fasting…my soul hates." What kind of fasting does God's soul "hate"? The kind that is out of touch with Him and His purpose, which is to "remove iniquities" from our souls and "diligently" to "seek judgment" and "deliverance" for those "suffering wrong."

God seeks to make Himself "known" to us, so that we "come, and reason together" with His justice and mercy. He does this in part through external disciplines like fasts and feasts. Because these disciplines bring us together, out of self-isolation, and also slow us down, in our disparate and distracting pursuits. But they are not ends in themselves, and they lose their meaning outside of God. The "end" that God pursues, in slowing us down through fasting and feasting/resting periods, is our communion with Him, our harmony with His love and mercy.

So let me not lose sight of the forest, which is the "big" picture of God's all-encompassing justice and mercy, for the trees, which are the fasting-rules. We "ought" to follow the latter, as our Lord tells us, "without neglecting" the former (Mt 23: 23). As I begin the salvific discipline of Lent, let me "come and reason together" with God as He calls me to, in heartfelt prayer, and in humble reliance on His grace, so He can make my sins "white as snow" in and with Him. Happy beginning of Lent!

Meal Plan (A): *Strict Fast Day with No Oil*
*TIP: Today cook a large pot of beans or lentils, bag one-meal portions, and freeze them so you can use them in your salads and meals throughout the week.

TUESDAY, 1st WEEK

GOD-GIVEN CHANGE

"And God said, 'Let there be lights in the firmament of the heavens to separate the day from the night; and let them be for signs and for seasons and for days and years, and let them be lights in the firmament of the heavens to give light upon the earth.' And it was so. And God made the two great lights, the greater light to rule the day, and the lesser light to rule the night; he made the stars also. And God set them in the firmament of the heavens to give light upon the earth, to rule over the day and over the night, and to separate the light from the darkness. And God saw that it was good. And there was evening and there was morning, a fourth day." (Gen 1: 14-19)

This is one of the readings for today, the second day of Lent. It redirects me, just like the rest of Lent, to the "basics" of my faith, which I tend to take for granted. Today I'm reminded of the basic, yet awe-inspiring fact that God created changeability and change. And He called it "good."

It is good for me that I experience God-given, physical transition and change all the time, which is beyond my control, – from night to day, from midday to evening, from one month to the next, from winter to spring, from youth to adulthood, and so on. Because total monotony in our physical world would feel like a window-less prison cell.

But God also gives me a capacity to change in ways I can choose, according to my free will. I can step into His light and grow in Him, or I can self-isolate and stay in the shadows, doing whatever it is I want to do over there, on my own. But the great, liberating fact is, I don't have to do that. There is light, and today I can step right into it, in some heartfelt prayer and contemplation of His word. Because "the light shines in the darkness," also in my darkness today, "and the darkness has not overcome it." (Jn 1: 5)

Meal Plan (A): *Strict Fast Day with No Oil*
*TIP: If you plan on going to confession at the end of this week, consider journaling; perhaps just a few lines about the pluses and minuses of your day, and where/how you want to do better.

WEDNESDAY, 1st WEEK

CRY OUT FOR DISCERNMENT

"For if you cry out for discernment, and lift up your voice for understanding; and if you seek it as silver, and search diligently for it as for treasures; then you will understand the fear of the Lord, and find the knowledge of God. For the Lord gives wisdom; and from his presence come knowledge and understanding, and he treasures up salvation for them that walk uprightly: he will protect their way;" (Prov 2: 3-7)

Discernment. Wisdom. Knowledge. Understanding. Are these the things I've been searching for "diligently, …as for treasures"? At times, yes. But I need to be reminded, again and again, that these essential gifts, without which my life becomes utterly unmanageable, come from God. I must not only ask Him for them, but "cry out" for them when need be. Because I desperately need God to nudge me in the right direction, despite the weaknesses and distortions in my own vision of things.

Let me re-connect with, and stay close to, Him today, especially when I don't know what I'm doing, or what to do next. Because "from his presence come knowledge and wisdom." Help me, Lord, do the next right thing today, in Your presence and grace. Amen!

Meal Plan (A): *Strict Fast Day with No Oil*
*TIP: Consider a "Midweek Treat" today (see Meal Plan), and check out the beautiful Lenten Liturgy of Presanctified Gifts, celebrated today for the first time this year, at a church near you!

THURSDAY, 1st WEEK

IDLENESS & PROCRASTINATION

"O Lord and Master of my life, grant me not the spirit of idleness (ἀργίας, праздности), despondency, lust of power, and idle talk (ἀργο-λογίας, праздно-словия)." (Lenten Prayer of St. Ephrem, part 1)

Here the "spirit of idleness" or "ἀργία" (from "ἀ-εργία," literally "not working" or "not doing") means the bad kinds of "not doing." There are also good kinds of "not doing" (праздность) at certain, appropriate times (праздники), because we all need an occasional break in order to be restored. But here idleness means "not doing" what I am supposed to be doing, and when I am supposed to be doing it, according to my "vocation" or calling from God, specifically out of an avoidance and/or neglect of "responsibility" (i.e., my "response-ability" or my "ability to respond" to God's call). One such type of idleness is procrastination, e.g., when I have a pile of papers to grade, but opt to clean my desk instead.

What causes me to befriend the "spirit of idleness," including procrastination? Several things: 1. self-reliance, when I'm attempting to carry my responsibilities on my own shoulders, without God; 2. The resulting fear (of both failure and success) regarding the task at hand, which is too much for me alone; and 3. A loss of vision/sense of my "vocation," due to all-of-the-above.

So this morning let me replace fear with faith, and self-reliance with God-reliance, so I don't get stuck in self-centered, fear-inspired circles. Let me re-focus and listen for God's call to me, that I may respond in humble usefulness to myself and others. "Thy will be done" with me today, O Lord, according to Your purpose, whether I like it right now or not. Amen!

Meal Plan (A): *Strict Fast Day with No Oil*
*TIP: For additional daily exercise, try praying the Lenten Prayer of St. Ephrem, with 3 great prostrations if you can, - once in the morning and once more before bed. And congratulations on almost completing the first week of Lent!

FRIDAY, 1st WEEK

GOD-FOCUSED HUNGER

"And Jesus, full of the Holy Spirit, returned from the Jordan, and was led by the Spirit for forty days in the wilderness, tempted by the devil. And he ate nothing in those days; and when they were ended, he was hungry. The devil said to him, 'If you are the Son of God, command this stone to become bread.' And Jesus answered him, 'It is written, 'Man shall not live by bread alone.'" (Lk 4: 1-4)

Jesus was, indeed, "hungry." He did, indeed, "need" something to eat. He also "could" provide bread for Himself in the wilderness, because this was within His power. Nonetheless, He rejects the devil's enticing suggestion, to turn a stone to bread. Why?

Because it's the devil's suggestion. And Christ is showing us that our God-given, physical needs, as well as our God-given powers, are not to be addressed outside God, as if they had a life of their own. We are called to train and exercise our needs and capacities in a God-focused way, as God wants, and not as the devil wants. "Asceticism," from the Greek word "ἄσκησις," meaning "exercise, practice, training," in which we now engage during Lent, is a way to train and direct our human needs and divine capacities toward God's purpose and will, with His purpose and will in mind. By becoming a little more hungry and vulnerable, through fasting, we become more attentive to how and when we respond to our various hungers, both physical and spiritual.

Let me let myself be a bit hungry today, in a God-focused manner. And when I eat, let me be attentive to "receiving" my food, rather than just taking it, according to a will that is not God's. *"Blessed are those who hunger and thirst for righteousness, for they will be satisfied."* (Mt 5: 6)

Meal Plan (A): *Strict Fast Day with No Oil*
*TIP: If you plan on going to confession this weekend, consider journaling today; perhaps just a few lines about the pluses and minuses of your day/few days, and where/how you want to do better. And treat yourself today to a Lenten Liturgy of Presanctified Gifts, celebrated today at a church near you!

SATURDAY, 1ˢᵗ WEEK (The Miracle of St. Theodore)

LORD OF THE SABBATH

"Again he entered the synagogue, and a man was there who had a withered hand. They watched him to see whether he would cure him on the sabbath, so that they might accuse him. And he said to the man who had the withered hand, 'Come forward (εἰς τὸ μέσον, into the middle).' Then he said to them, 'Is it lawful to do good or to do harm on the sabbath, to save life or to kill?' But they were silent. He looked around at them with anger; he was grieved at their hardness of heart and said to the man, 'Stretch out your hand.' He stretched it out, and his hand was restored. The Pharisees went out and immediately conspired with the Herodians against him, how to destroy him.'" (Mk 3: 1-6)

So the Pharisees have murder in their hearts, seeking "to destroy" Jesus, – and this unlawful desire they embrace on the sabbath. At the same time, they object to our Lord's insistence on "doing good" on the sabbath, like healing the man with the withered hand. This is why they are silent, when He asks them, *"Is it lawful to do good or to do harm on the sabbath, to save life or to kill?"* The Pharisees have so enslaved themselves (and others) to the external forms of the Law that they have no room in their hearts for its Spirit, Who is "Lord of the Sabbath" (cf. Mk 2: 28).

On this Saturday at the end of the first week of Lent, let me re-connect with the Lord of the Sabbath, opening my heart to His humble presence. However "good" or "bad" I am at following our fasting rules, let me not shut out His mercy, through formalistic demands of myself and/or others. I reach out to God, as one with a withered hand, unable "to do good" but by His grace.

Meal Plan (B): *Fast Day with Oil*
*TIP: This morning "koliva" (boiled wheat & honey) is blessed after Divine Liturgy, so have some if you can get to church, and be blessed! And congratulations on completing the first week! Try to rest a bit and have a Weekend Treat, so you're refreshed for the upcoming second week.

1ˢᵗ SUNDAY OF LENT (of Orthodoxy)

I SAW YOU

"The next day Jesus decided to go to Galilee. And he found Philip and said to him, 'Follow me.' Now Philip was from Bethsaida, the city of Andrew and Peter. Philip found Nathanael, and said to him, 'We have found him of whom Moses in the law and also the prophets wrote, Jesus of Nazareth, the son of Joseph.' Nathanael said to him, 'Can anything good come out of Nazareth?' Philip said to him, 'Come and see.' Jesus saw Nathanael coming to him, and said of him, 'Behold, an Israelite indeed, in whom is no guile!' Nathanael said to him, 'How do you know me?' Jesus answered him, 'Before Philip called you, when you were under the fig tree, I saw you.' Nathanael answered him, 'Rabbi, you are the Son of God! You are the King of Israel!'" (Jn 1: 43-49)

Nathaniel is weak in his reasoning, when he says, "Can anything good come out of Nazareth?" – as if nothing "good" can come out of a poor and insignificant town. He also seems to have a hard time accepting good news. But he is not insincere or hypocritical. And our Lord immediately praises this good in Nathaniel; the fact that in him there is "no guile," rather than point out his weaknesses. But Nathaniel, apparently, also has a hard time accepting praise, deflecting it with a question, "How do you know me?" So he's a hard nut to crack. Nathaniel does "come and see" the Lord, but "seeing" Christ was not enough for him.

It is only when Christ reveals to Nathaniel, "I saw you," that Nathaniel drops his defenses and professes Jesus as Teacher (rabbi), Son of God, and King of Israel. Because for many of us who are on the sidelines of faith, what wins us over to Christ is not "us" seeing "Him." Because He is revealing Himself all the time, but we may not have the eyes to see that. What wins us over, in an encounter with Christ, is receiving the assurance that "He" does, indeed, see "us," and know us, as we are, in our strengths and weaknesses. So let me "come and see" Christ, that I don't miss out on being seen, and known, by Him.

Meal Plan (B): *Fast Day with Oil*
*TIP: This morning holy icons are celebrated at Divine Liturgy, as we celebrate "seeing" the incarnate Lord and also His saints on holy icons. "Come and see" for yourself, if you can get to church, and be seen! Let yourself rest a bit and have a Weekend Treat, so you're refreshed for the upcoming second week.

2nd Week of Lent
MONDAY, 2nd Week

A LIGHT BURDEN

"Come to me, all who labor and are heavy laden, and I will give you rest. Take my yoke upon you, and learn from me; for I am meek and humble in heart, and you will find rest for your souls. For my yoke is easy, and my burden is light." (Mt 11: 28-30)

As I enter the second week of Lent, I'm wondering whether Lent itself is part of the "burden" or "yoke" Christ is talking about. Is it?

Well, it can be, if it is "easy" and "light." Because that is how our Lord defines His "yoke" and "burden." He invites us to take these up in "meekness" and "humility in heart." So, if I take up Lent in meekness and humility, picking up its simple tools without needlessly debating how/whether they're right for me, I find that Lent brings me out of my own brand of "labor" and being "heavy laden," with its self-imposed "musts" and "needs." Lent gives me "rest" from my usual routine, offering me a routine not self-imposed, and filled with meaning and purpose. It is a meaning and purpose above and beyond my immediate stress, the meaning and purpose of which is not always clear.

This Monday I once again embrace the meaning and purpose of Lent, which is a re-focusing on a God-centered life, a "change of mind" (metanoia) according to a humble self-acceptance, according to my God-given possibilities or "vocation." Lord, renew in me a right Spirit today, and help me learn from You, that I may find rest for my soul. Amen!

Meal Plan (A): *Strict Fast Day with No Oil*
Meal Plan (B): *Fast Day with Oil – for Older Calendar in 2021, celebrating The 40 Martyrs of Sebaste today (March 22)*
*NOTE: Today on the Older Calendar, a Liturgy of Presanctified Gifts is celebrated as it's the feast of the 40 Martyrs; wine and oil are allowed.

For more on the saints and church-services of today, tune in to the "Morning Coffee" audio-podcast at **patreon.com/sistervassa**.
And re-connect with fellow Healthy*Fast*ers!

TUESDAY, 2nd WEEK

DRINKING FROM MY OWN WELL

"Drink water from your own cistern, flowing water from your own well. Should your springs be scattered abroad, streams of water in the streets? Let them be for yourself alone, and not for strangers with you. Let your fountain be blessed, and rejoice in the wife of your youth... Let her affection fill you at all times with delight, be infatuated always with her love. Why should you be infatuated, my son, with a loose woman and embrace the bosom of an adventuress? For a man's ways are before the eyes of the Lord, and he (the Lord) watches all his paths." (Prov 5: 15-21)

Today, in our Internet Age, I can "drink water" from many available "wells," and also "scatter" my own all over the place. What does this mean? It means that I am easily distracted from my own vocation and tradition; from being of service and usefulness in the specific ways I am given, according to the upbringing, education, talents, people, situations, and other gifts I am given. I might forget even to speak with the person/s right in front of me, if my nose is in the little screen on my phone, constantly distracted "elsewhere."

Lent offers me a kind of "crash-course" in re-identifying with "the wife of my youth." (And yes, I realize the analogy is an awkward one, since I happen to be a woman. But please just work with me here.) The "wife of my youth" is my own Tradition, which has nurtured me, and cared for me, and continues to be there for me, reminding me of who I am, even at the times when I've looked "elsewhere." So today let me drink "from my own well," and re-focus on the abundant blessings I have in the here and now. Lord, help me be grateful and useful today, on the immediate paths You have set before me. Amen!

Meal Plan (A): *Strict Fast Day with No Oil*
*TIP: If your fast-days are beginning to feel harder, try integrating a mid-morning or mid-afternoon "treat," which is small enough to have every day without throwing you off your plan, but also a bit of a "reward" for sticking to it today. For example, a small extra-dry oatmilk cappucino sprinkled with cinnamon, or some other small snack you will look forward to.

WEDNESDAY, 2nd Week

THE FAITH OF THE ATHEIST

"Now faith is the assurance of things hoped for, the conviction of things not seen. For by it the men of old received divine approval. By faith we understand that the world was created by the word of God, so that what is seen was made out of things which do not appear." (Hebr 11: 1-3)

I'm thinking that the atheist view is also a faith, because it is a "conviction of things not seen." Because the atheist has "not seen" that God does not, indeed, exist. The atheist "faith" is not, however, an "assurance of things hoped for." It is a choice, rather, to close the door on all hope and on the ambivalences of mystery. Hence atheism tends to be sad, because it lacks hope, and it tends to be dull, because it lacks mystery. It is limited to man-made "understanding" like philosophy or mythology, while missing out on "divine approval," i.e., the voice of God to us.

Today I choose, once again, to embrace the ambivalence "of things hoped for." I embrace the adventure of mystery, both in my relationship with God and with others, all "made out of things that do not appear." May I be mindful today "of things not seen," by the grace of His word.

Meal Plan (B): *Fast Day with Oil*, **for New Calendar Forefeast of Annunciation (March 24) in 2021**
Meal Plan (A): *Strict Fast Day with No Oil – on Older Calendar*
*TIP: Consider a "Midweek Treat" today (see Meal Plan), and check out the beautiful Lenten Liturgy of Presanctified Gifts, celebrated on Lenten Wednesdays at a church near you!

THURSDAY, 2nd WEEK

HOW SHALL THIS BE?

"…And Mary said to the angel, 'How shall this be, since I have no husband?' And the angel said to her, 'The Holy Spirit will come upon you, and the power of the Most High will overshadow you; therefore the child to be born will be called holy, the Son of God. And behold, your kinswoman Elizabeth in her old age has also conceived a son; and this is the sixth month with her who was called barren. For with God nothing will be impossible.' And Mary said, 'Behold, I am the handmaid of the Lord; let it be to me according to your word.' And the angel departed from her." (Lk 1: 34-38)

The "mystery" or "sacrament" of the Virgin Birth, that is, of the Most Holy Virgin's "vocation," raises an understandable, human question: "How shall this be…?" It is similar to the question(s) raised by Nicodemus in John 3, when our Lord talks to him about another "mystery" or "sacrament," of Baptism. Nicodemus asks: "How can a man be born when he is old? Can he enter a second time into his mother's womb and be born?" (Jn 3: 4) And our Lord's response to Nicodemus, like the angel's response to the Theotokos's question, refers to the Holy Spirit, with Whom "nothing will be impossible." As Christ explains to Nicodemus, "…Do not marvel that I said to you, 'You must be born anew/from above.' The Spirit blows where he wills, and you hear the sound of him, but you do not know whence it comes or whither it goes; so it is with every one who is born of the Spirit." (Jn 3: 7-8) …But Nicodemus, somewhat differently from the Theotokos, continues to ask, "How can this be?" (Jn 3: 9)

When I'm confronted with God's "mysteries," including the unusual circumstances of our lives during a worldwide pandemic, I might find myself asking, "How shall this be?" But let me be reminded that God, the Holy Spirit, does "blow" us in unexpected directions at times, as He wills, and that in Him "nothing will be impossible," if only we let ourselves be carried by Him. So in the timeless words of Bob Dylan: "The answer, my friend, is blowing in the Wind; the answer is blowing in the Wind." Happy Annunciation, (if you're NC and reading this in 2021), and Older Calendar-friends, - Thursday of the second week!

Meal Plan (C): *Fast Day with Fish*, **and Divine Liturgy is celebrated, on New Calendar Annunciation (March 25) in 2021**
Meal Plan (A): *Strict Fast Day with No Oil*, **if you're OC and not celebrating Annunciation**

FRIDAY, 2nd Week

IDLE TALK

"O Lord and Master of my life, grant me not the spirit of idleness (ἀργίας, праздности), despondency, lust of power, and idle talk / idle words (ἀργο-λογίας, праздно-словия)." (Lenten Prayer of St. Ephrem, part 1)

It is important for us to talk and to share with one another our thoughts, sorrows, joys, and so on. No doubt about it. In fact I think we don't do enough of that today, when we are so often "alone together," even as a family, with each member staring into his or her computer/phone while sitting at the same table. Nonetheless, there is such a thing as "idle talk/words," so let me reflect on that a bit. What is it?

Just like "idleness" (ἀργία, from ἀ-ἐργία, or "not doing") means "not doing" what I am supposed to be doing, how, when and why I am supposed to be doing it, so does my "idle" use of words (ἀργο-λογία), whether spoken, written, or typed on my computer, mean my "not saying" what I am supposed to be saying, how, when and why I am supposed to be saying it, according to my vocation. So, "idle words" involve the inappropriate and untimely use of words, as well as their use with the wrong motivation. "Idle words" are always unconstructive, unproductive ones, which do more harm than good both to myself and others.

What are some of the "wrong" motivations for using words, and why are they harmful? I can, for example, "over-talk" about my certain aspirations or problems, out of self-assertion, self-justification, or self-pity. The harm in that is, I may be avoiding the silent contemplation of these issues; avoiding listening for the answers God may be sending me toward their further resolution, either through other people or otherwise. So I am blocking out the answers through my own words. I can similarly over-talk to God, as Christ warns us: *"And in praying do not heap up empty phrases as the Gentiles do; for they think that they will be heard for their many words..."* (Mt 6: 7)

So let me be reminded today of something I recently read (in the "Harvard Business Review," if you want to know). It's a bit of advice very useful in matters both practical and spiritual: "Silence is a greatly underestimated source of power… In silence, it can be easier to reach the truth." Let me stop my own words, when they cease to be of service, and become a bit more teachable, in silence and openness to God's voice in my life.

Meal Plan (B): *Fast Day with Oil*, **on NC-Afterfeast of Annunciation/Synaxis of Archangel Gabriel (March 26) in 2021**
Meal Plan (A): *Strict Fast Day with No Oil*, **on OC**
*TIP: Treat yourself to a nice walk in the fresh air today, if you haven't been doing that daily, and congratulations on almost-completing the second week! The beautiful Lenten Liturgy of Presanctified Gifts is celebrated today (on both calendars).

SATURDAY, 2ⁿᵈ WEEK (of the reposed)

THE LIGHT OF LIFE

"Again Jesus spoke to them, saying, 'I am the light of the world; he who follows me will not walk in darkness, but will have the light of life (τὸ φῶς τῆς ζωῆς).'" (Jn 8: 12)

What is "light"? In physical terms it is that which enables us to see. In theological terms it is God Himself, whose presence enables me to see things as they are, rather than how I wish or imagine them to be.

Let me not walk in darkness today, because I don't have to. "God is the Lord and has revealed Himself to us." (Ps 117: 27) Blessed is He Who comes, and blessed are we who receive Him, and choose to walk in His light and lightness.

Meal Plan (B): *Fast Day with Oil*
*NOTE: In Russian Orthodox and some other churches, this is a Memorial Saturday, when the deceased are commemorated. In Greek Orthodox parishes, Lenten Saturdays are usually dedicated to chanting (a part of) the Akathist-hymn to the Theotokos. Try to rest a bit today and have a Weekend Treat, so you're refreshed for the upcoming second week. And congratulations on completing the second week!

2nd SUNDAY OF LENT (of St. Gregory Palamas)

WE SHOULD HAVE SUCH A HIGH PRIEST

"For it was fitting that we should have such a High Priest (τοιοῦτος...ἀρχιερεύς), *holy, blameless, unstained, separated from sinners, exalted above the heavens. He has no need, like high priests* (ὥσπερ οἱ ἀρχιερεῖς), *to offer sacrifices daily, first for his own sins and then for those of the people; he did this once for all* (ἐφάπαξ) *when he offered up himself. Indeed, the law appoints men in their weakness as high priests, but the word of the oath, which came later than the law, appoints a Son who has been made perfect for ever."*
(Hebr 7: 26-28)

We do, indeed, have many priests and "high" priests (e.g., bishops, archbishops, metropolitans, etc.). These are "men" appointed "in their weakness," and not "separated from sinners." But we only have One "such" High Priest, Who had no need to offer up "for" Himself, because He had no sin. He offered up, rather, Himself, and did so "once and for all" (ἐφάπαξ). And it is the human-divine person of Jesus Christ, with His unique, high-priestly ministry to all of us, that continues to be the Source of power and meaning for the "other" priests and high priests. Our "other" priests and high priests are no more, and indeed no less, than participants in a priesthood that is His alone.

I need this reminder every now and then, of Him Who is the basis of all our liturgical rites and rituals, lest I slip into some wrong approach to church-going. One such "wrong" approach is a subtle consumerism, as if I am "fixing myself," as I see fit (whether I decide to approach confession, communion, and so on). Another false approach would be a focus/dependency on the personalities in church, as if the whole enterprise called "Church" was about human beings fixing or serving me. The power and "meaning of it all" remains, ever-perfectly, ever-stably, One "separated from sinners" and "exalted above the heavens." Today let me give up, once again, any attempts to "fix myself" or "be fixed" by human help alone. Even as I gratefully receive the ministry and help of priests in my church, I surrender to the will of One far greater than all of us, our Lord Jesus Christ, for it is "fitting," as St. Paul says, "that we should have such a High Priest."

Meal Plan (B): *Fast Day with Oil*
*TIP: This morning at Divine Liturgy we celebrate a great teacher/practitioner of "The Jesus Prayer," St. Gregory Palamas. Let's focus on heartfelt prayer, and also get some physical rest this Sunday and have a Weekend Treat, as we approach Week 3 with renewed energy!

3rd Week of Lent
MONDAY, 3rd Week

HUMILITY, AN ELUSIVE THING

"But grant unto me, Your servant, a spirit of chastity (σωφροσύνης, whole-mindedness, цело-мудрия)*, humility* (ταπεινοφροσύνης, humble-mindedness, смиренно-мудрия)*, patience and love."* (Lenten Prayer of St. Ephrem, part 2)

Humility is an elusive kind of thing, hard to define. It is also easy to mistake some "humility-counterfeit" for actual humility. For example, I might imagine I am being "humble," while actually escaping responsibility, according to my vocation, or donning a mask I have concocted, just not to be who I am called to be in my God-given place, time, and identity. As G. K. Chesterton famously noted, *"What we suffer from today is humility in the wrong place. Modesty has moved from the organ of ambition and settled upon the organ of conviction, where it was never meant to be. A man was meant to be doubtful about himself, but undoubting about the truth."*

The Lenten Prayer of St. Ephrem tells me three helpful things about humility: 1. It is good for me to ask for it, so I should desire it; 2. It is a "spirit," more specifically, it is an energy of the Holy Spirit, to which I open up, rather than something I should or can muster up from inside me; and 3. It is a "mindset" (ταπεινο-φροσύνη, humble-mindedness, смиренно- мудрие) or "approach" to things, which involves a way of thinking. When I am "in" the grace of humble-mindedness, and the grace of humble-mindedness is "in" me, I find myself wisely able to "duck under the wave," in the Holy Spirit, when need be – of the dangerous wave or calamity that happens to come my way. So, humility is a "ducking under the wave," in the warm shelter and loving care of the Holy Spirit, rather than asserting my own, Spirit-less response to things. This does not always mean being silent, nor does it mean "being a doormat." It means asserting His energies, rather than my own. He becomes greater, and I become less. (cf. Jn 3: 30)

Today let me open up to God and His Spirit, staying close to Him, so that my response to situations, things, and people around me are softened and salted by humility, in His, and not my, wisdom. *"But grant unto me, Your servant, a Spirit of humble-mindedness."* Amen!

Meal Plan (A): *Strict Fast Day with No Oil*
*TIP: Today try making a big pot of soup, like creamed broccoli & cauliflower with fresh dill and lemon (and/or fresh ginger), which you can have for several meals in this upcoming week, with some cooked buckwheat thrown in, or on the side.

For more on the saints and church-services of today, tune in to the "Morning Coffee" audio-podcast at **patreon.com/sistervassa**.
And re-connect with fellow Healthy*Fast*ers!

TUESDAY, 3rd WEEK

THE FORTY DAYS

"In the six hundredth year of Noah's life, in the second month, on the seventeenth day of the month, on that day all the fountains of the great deep burst forth, and the windows of the heavens were opened. And rain fell upon the earth forty days and forty nights." (Gen 7: 11- 12)

Here's a strange thought. These "forty days and forty nights," mentioned in our Church's reading for today, during Lent, remind me of the 40 days of Lent. But is that really strange, to connect these two?

No, I don't think so. Because Scripture, along with other parts of Tradition, like Lent, is handed down to me, so I can make connections and "recognize" One-and-the-Same God working and speaking through it, yesterday and today. Certain symbols, like "forty days," repeat themselves here and there throughout Tradition, revealing a common language and common Source of that language, namely, God.

So, to get to my point, today I'm "connecting" the "forty days and forty nights" of rain falling upon the earth in The Great Flood with what is happening now, during Great Lent. In The Great Flood, God *"blotted out every living thing that was upon the face of the ground, man and animals and creeping things and birds of the air; they were blotted out from the earth. Only Noah was left, and those that were with him in the ark."* (Gen 7: 23) Now, during Lent, we are brought together in a special, extra-focused way in the ark that is the Church, experiencing a "flood" of God's grace in the intensified prayers, fasting, and other rituals of Lent. This "flood" is meant to "blot out" from my life all that has ceased to serve God's purpose. So I can re-focus, with others huddled together in our "ark," on His purpose, and then move on in a God-centered manner. Lord, give me shelter today in Your ark, and blot out "every living thing," still living in me, which has ceased to serve You. Amen!

Meal Plan (A): *Strict Fast Day with No Oil*
*TIP: If you're planning to go to confession at the mid-point of Lent (on the upcoming Sunday of the Cross), consider journaling, noting the ups and downs of your day, and where/how you want to do better.

WEDNESDAY, 3rd Week

INTERNET PORN, THE "SECRET BREAD"

"A foolish and bold woman, who knows not modesty, comes to want a morsel. She sits at the doors of her house, on a seat openly in the streets, calling to passers by, and to those that are going right on their ways; saying, Whoever is most senseless of you, let him turn aside to me; and I exhort those that want prudence, saying, Take and enjoy secret bread, and the sweet water of theft. But one knows that mighty men die by her, and that one falls in with a snare of hell. But hasten away, delay not in the place, neither fix your eye upon her: for thus shall you go through strange water; but do abstain from strange water, and drink not of a strange fountain, that you may live long, and years of life may be added to you." (Prov 9:13-18, Septuagint-translation)

So forgive the awkward topic. But this passage from Proverbs is part of our Church's reading for today, the third Wednesday of Lent, and it sheds some helpful light, I think, on the "secret bread" and secret torment of many today, also among Orthodox Christians, – and that is, Internet pornography. Just recently I heard from an Orthodox priest that he hears quite a bit about this issue from Orthodox people at confession.

I think the above-quoted passage, while it was written over two millennia ago and wasn't talking about modern-day Internet-pornography, does expose its ugly "thinking" and spirit. Scripture is telling me here, this is "secret bread" and "strange water." It is both "bread" and "water," so it does satisfy a certain hunger, and quench a certain thirst. But it is "strange water," as well as "sweet water of theft," which is not healthy for me, or appropriate to my actual needs. It is an imposter, and a surrogate for fulfilling my God-given desires and drives. I am, indeed, given desires, also physical ones, from God, as is any human being, that I may grow and be useful to others and myself. So for a person of faith, desires and drives are to be discerned and channelled according to one's own, true vocation, and not according to the whims of "a foolish and bold woman," like Internet porn, who simply "comes to want a morsel" of us. I am not called to waste my will on imposters.

So let me not "delay in the place, neither fix my eye" on "the foolish and bold woman" that is Internet-pornography, that wants to "turn me aside to her" and waste my God-given desires and energies at her "strange fountain." And if she has lured me into sharing her dirty little secrets, let me expose this at confession, that I may "share" with her no more. O Lord, I turn my energies and will over to Your care today, that I may be useful to You, myself, and others, rather than waste my time. Amen!

Meal Plan (A): *Strict Fast Day with No Oil*
*TIP: Have a Midweek Treat today and take heart, as we've almost reached the middle of our journey! If you're planning to go to confession at the mid-point of Lent (on the upcoming Sunday of the Cross), consider journaling, noting the ups and downs of your day, and where/how you want to do better.

THURSDAY, 3rd WEEK

OUR DAILY BREAD

"Give us this day our daily (τὸν ἐπιούσιον) *bread, and forgive us our trespasses, as we forgive those who trespass against us..."* (Mt 6: 11-12)

Yesterday I reflected on an unhealthy, deadly kind of "bread" that is Internet porn. Today I'd like to reflect on the vital, essential, "daily bread," suitable to our nature both now and in the life to come (according to the many explanations one finds in the Fathers, of the term "τὸν ἐπιούσιον"), which we are called to ask for and desire. One of the great things about Lent, I find, is that it teaches me to pay closer attention to my "food-choices," both physical and spiritual.

As far as physical "bread" goes, let me gratefully note that God provides it for me today. It includes the entirety of my physical needs, like food, shelter, clothing, technology, etc. Gratitude steers me away from taking this "bread" for granted, or snatching up too much of it, or desiring "more," or desiring what others have, when I actually have enough. And forgiveness helps maintain my peace with my material situation, if anyone else "trespasses" against, or takes away, any of my "bread."

As far as healthy and vital spiritual "bread" goes, let me note that I easily lose sight of it altogether, overindulging in the wrong kind. I often allow myself to be fed "too much information" from news-sources or other media. I may be entirely exhausted and famished, without the essential "daily bread" I need, and not even notice it.

So today let me take pause, and take care of my health, both physical and spiritual. Let me re-connect with the Giver of Life and open up to His nurturing presence and grace, so abundantly on offer today, and every day. I take a bit of time for some deep, prayerful reading as well, that I may be nourished and strengthened through life-giving words, rather than exhausting and confusing ones. "Give us this day our daily bread, and forgive us our trespasses, as we forgive those who trespass against us." Amen!

Meal Plan (A): *Strict Fast Day with No Oil*

FRIDAY, 3rd Week

THE SIXTH & NINTH HOUR

"And when the sixth hour had come, there was darkness over the whole land until the ninth hour. And at the ninth hour Jesus cried with a loud voice, 'E'lo-i, E'lo-i, la'ma sabach-tha'ni?' which means, 'My God, my God, why have you forsaken me?' And some of the bystanders hearing it said, 'Behold, he is calling Elijah.' And one ran and, filling a sponge full of vinegar, put it on a reed and gave it to him to drink, saying, 'Wait, let us see whether Elijah will come to take him down.' And Jesus uttered a loud cry, and breathed his last. And the curtain of the temple was torn in two, from top to bottom. And when the centurion, who stood facing him, saw that he thus breathed his last, he said, 'Truly this man was the Son of God!'" (Mk 15: 33-39)

On this third Friday of Lent, I'd like to remember that Friday over two millennia ago, when things so radically changed between us and God. The "curtain of the temple," which separated the Holy of Holies, God's earthly dwelling-place, from the rest of the temple where human beings dwelt, was "torn in two." The separation between us and God was being overcome in Christ's death. He had taken on our "sin," which separated us from God, and its consequence, death, darkness, and even despair, in order to "trample" all that and bring us out of it, in Him.

How is it that He brings "us" out of it, and not only Himself? Because He shares our humanity, our human nature, having become man. We share an underlying oneness, a connection, from human being to human being, both physical and spiritual, although it is easy to lose sight of this fact amidst our divisions. Our spiritual connection is our one-and-only Creator, God's Spirit Who breathed life into us. Our physical connection, already obvious in the scientific fact that our genetic make-up is 99.9 percent identical, is made profoundly more intimate in the Body of Christ, of which He invites us to partake in Holy Communion.

Today in my "sixth hour" (i.e., midday) and in my "ninth hour" (3 o'clock in the afternoon) let me take pause and remember the "darkness over the whole land," the "loud voice" of the God Man, crying out in our despair, and the "tearing in two" of that curtain of separation, through my Lord's "last" breath. *"In the ninth hour, You tasted death in the flesh for our sake, O Christ God. Put also to death our carnal mind* (thinking according to the flesh, τῆς σαρκὸς ἡμῶν τὸ φρόνημα, плоти нашея мудрование), *and save us!"* (Byzantine Troparion of the Ninth Hour)

Meal Plan (A): *Strict Fast Day with No Oil*

SATURDAY, 3rd WEEK (of the reposed)

HE ROSE AND CAME HOME

"And as he passed on, he saw Levi the son of Alphaeus sitting at the tax office, and he said to him, 'Follow me.' And he rose and followed him. And as he sat at table in his house, many tax collectors and sinners were sitting with Jesus and his disciples; for there were many who followed him. And the scribes and the Pharisees, when they saw that he was eating with sinners and tax collectors, said to his disciples, 'Why does he eat with tax collectors and sinners?' And when Jesus heard it, he said to them, 'Those who are well (οἱ ἰσχύοντες) *have no need of a physician, but those who are sick* (οἱ κακῶς ἔχοντες); *I came not to call the righteous, but sinners to repentance* (εἰς μετάνοιαν)." (Mk 2: 14-17)

So Levi, one of the "sinners" in this picture, was called to "repentance" ("metanoia," a change of mind, change of focus). What did "repentance" look like, in his case? First, Levi "rose" from where he was sitting. Then he "followed" Christ, Who led him back into his own home. And there Levi "ate" with his fellow-tax-collectors and sinners, together with the Lord.

Lord, I am, once again, "in need of a physician" today, where I am sitting, outside my true "home." So once again I hear Your call: I "rise" and let You lead me back where I belong, "at table" and in fellowship with You and my fellow-sinners.

Meal Plan (B): *Fast Day with Oil*
*NOTE: In Russian Orthodox and some other churches, this is a Memorial Saturday, when the deceased are commemorated. In Greek Orthodox parishes, Lenten Saturdays are usually dedicated to chanting (a part of) the Akathist-hymn to the Theotokos. And coming up at Sunday-matins of this weekend (celebrated Saturday evening in Russian churches and Sunday morning in Greek churches) is the Veneration of the Cross! Don't miss it!

3rd SUNDAY OF LENT (Veneration of the Cross)

BEING ALONE vs. BEARING MUCH FRUIT

"And he called to him the multitude with his disciples, and said to them, 'If any man wants to come after me, let him deny himself and take up his cross and follow me. For whoever would save his life/soul (τὴν ψυχὴν αὐτοῦ) will lose it; and whoever loses his life/soul for my sake and the gospel's will save it. For what does it profit a man, to gain the whole world and forfeit his life/soul? For what can a man give in return for his life/soul?'" (Mk 8: 34- 37)

This doesn't make much sense, this talk about "losing" my "life/soul" in order to "save" it,– does it? Well, it does, if I remember that our Lord distinguishes between two kinds of "life/soul": 1. the kind we all have whether we want it or not, just by being born of our physical parents; and 2. The kind we can embrace "if we want to come after Him," denying a self-isolated existence outside of Him, and joining Him on the life-giving journey of the Cross. "Truly, truly, I say to you," He says on another occasion, *"unless a grain of wheat falls into the earth and dies, it remains alone; but if it dies, it bears much fruit. He who loves his life/soul loses it, and he who hates his life/soul in this world will keep it for eternal life."* (Jn 12: 24-25)

So let me proceed now, having venerated His cross at this mid-point of Lent, onwards and forwards to the next half of the cross-carrying adventure towards Pascha. Let me "lose" some more, of that which is not good for me, that I might "bear much fruit" as God wills, as I walk through my immediate responsibilities in His light and lightness. "Thy will be done" with me today, O Lord, that I not "remain alone," but "bear much fruit."

Meal Plan (B): *Fast Day with Oil*
*NOTE: Today at Divine Liturgy we venerate the Lord's cross, brought out in the center of the church. And throughout the upcoming 4th week of Lent, we continue to venerate it as a source of consolation and strength in the middle of our Lenten journey. Let's also get some physical rest this Sunday and have a Weekend Treat, as we enter Week 4 with renewed energy!

4th Week of Lent
MONDAY, 4th WEEK

EXTERNAL & INTERNAL BEAUTY

"As a ring in the snout of a pig, so is beauty in an ill-minded woman." (Prov 11: 22, Septuagint-translation)

Wow, that's harsh. But wait a minute, and let's think about what this passage says about physical beauty in human beings. Because it is talking about physical beauty in a person, – not only a woman, – whose internal disposition ("mind") is "ill." If you want to argue with that interpretation, and insist that this passage refers only to women, then go ahead and argue that the very first words of the Psalter, *"Blessed is the man…"* (Ps 1: 1), refer only to "men." If you will not argue that, then let's dispense with gender-specifics and talk about physical beauty in people in general.

Physical "beauty" in human beings attracts us to them, at a first glance, if we are not blind. But if we proceed to discover they are "ill-minded" in some way, then the contrast between their external appearance and their inner character ("mind") is particularly off-putting. Like "a ring in the snout of a pig." It isn't very "fair" to beautiful people, I suppose, but that is the way it is.

In our time of relative affluence, with our access to modern-day medicine, beauty-products, fitness-clubs, and healthy food, I think many of us have the opportunity to be more or less "beautiful" physically. But let us be reminded today, – if we do enjoy this gift of physical beauty and care for it, – of an ancient, simple wisdom from Holy Scripture. And that is, that physical beauty in a human being is not meant to be out of harmony with his/her spiritual beauty. Let me care for my inner "mind," that it not be "ill" but aligned with God, the Source of Beauty, in heartfelt prayer, contemplation of His word, and self-examination. Let me not neglect that, even as I take care of my physical health in a responsible way. Lord, help me keep things in perspective, that I may be healthy and beautiful in Your eyes. Amen!

Meal Plan (A): *Strict Fast Day with No Oil*
*TIP: This week we might venerate the cross at home, and decorate it with a bunch of fresh flowers. For OC-folks in 2021 the Annunciation is this Wednesday, so fasting will be mitigated for most of the week.

TUESDAY, 4th WEEK

GOD'S MANY SIGNS

"And the Lord God said to Noah, This is the sign of the covenant which I set between me and you, and between every living creature which is with you for perpetual generations. I set my rainbow in the cloud, and it shall be for a sign of covenant between me and the earth. And it shall be when I gather clouds upon the earth, that my rainbow shall be seen in the cloud. And I will remember my covenant, which is between me and you, and between every living soul in all flesh, and there shall no longer be water for a flood, so as to blot out all flesh." (Gen 9: 12-15)

So, a "rainbow in a cloud" is a special "sign of covenant," of a certain kind of agreement, understanding, or, simply put, "connection" that God has with us. Really there are countless "signs" in God's created world, which point us to Him as our common Creator, if we have the eyes to see. But we don't always have those eyes, as Simon and Garfunkel note in their brilliant song, "My Little Town": *"And after it rains, there's a rainbow, / And all of the colors are black, / It's not that the colors aren't there, / It's just imagination they lack, / Everything's the same back / In my little town."*

Today I'm reminded that God has His "signs" all over the place, as the Holy Spirit continues to "rain" and pour out His mercy most abundantly on "my little town." Everything is never "the same," from day to day, in the abundance of "colors" God shows me in the people, places and things He brings my way. Let me be both grateful and teachable today, that I can learn more about His presence and grace in our midst.

Meal Plan (A): *Strict Fast Day with No Oil – on New Calendar*
Meal Plan (B): *Fast Day with Oil – for Older Calendar Forefeast of Annunciation*
*TIP: OC-folks, prepare for tomorrow's great feast of the Annunciation; get flowers to place next to an icon of the Mother of God (in your home and/or in church), and buy some fish, because tomorrow you can have fish!

WEDNESDAY, 4th WEEK

UNREFLECTING FAITH

"In the sixth month the angel Gabriel was sent from God to a city of Galilee named Nazareth, to a virgin betrothed to a man whose name was Joseph, of the house of David; and the virgin's name was Mary. And he came to her and said, 'Hail, O full of grace (κεχαριτωμένη), the Lord is with you! Blessed are you among women!' But she was greatly troubled at the saying, and considered in her mind what sort of greeting this might be." (Lk 1: 26-29)

Mary was not an un-reflecting kind of person. She was "greatly troubled" by, and "considered in her mind" what in the world an angel, – yes, an angel, no less, – was talking about. She needed to know more, because the "greeting" made no sense in the context of Mary's life-experience thus far.

I'm thinking about this today, because I just read something that disturbed me in the works of the famous psychologist, Karl Jung, about us church-people often having "un-reflecting faith." This is what Jung observes: "The Churches stand for traditional and collective convictions which in the case of many of their adherents are no longer based on their own inner experience but on un-reflecting faith, which is notoriously apt to disappear as soon as one begins thinking about it." I was disturbed by Jung's observation, because I think he is right. I mean, it seems to me he is right as far as we, the people of my Church today, are concerned.

I'm consoled, however, by the example of the Blessed Among Women, in those early times of our "traditional and collective convictions," when the Holy Virgin was being introduced to them. She does "consider in her mind," and have questions, but also has an open heart to the replies of God's messenger, Gabriel. Let me also not hesitate today, to "consider in my mind" what it is God is telling me through His many messengers, including the people and situations He sends my way. *Most Holy Theotokos, save us!*

Meal Plan (A): *Strict Fast Day with No Oil – on New Calendar*
Meal Plan (C): *Fast Day with Fish, and Divine Liturgy is celebrated for Older Calendar Annunciation 2021, on April 7*

For more on the saints and church-services of today, tune in to the "Morning Coffee" audio-podcast at **patreon.com/sistervassa**.
And re-connect with fellow Healthy*Fast*ers!

THURSDAY, 4th WEEK

PLACING HOPE IN FALSEHOOD

"Therefore hear the word of the Lord, afflicted people, and rulers of the people that are in Jerusalem. Because you have said, We have made a covenant with Hades, and agreements with death; if the rushing storm should pass, it shall not come upon us: we have made falsehood our hope, and by falsehood shall we be protected: Therefore thus says the Lord, even the Lord, Behold, I lay for the foundations of Sion a costly stone, a choice, a corner-stone, a precious stone, for its foundations; and he that believes on him shall by no means be ashamed. And I will cause judgment to be for hope, and my compassion shall be for just measures, and you that trust vainly in falsehood shall fall: for the storm shall by no means pass by you, except it also take away your covenant of death, and your trust in Hades shall by no means stand: if the rushing storm should come upon you, you shall be beaten down by it." (Is 28: 14-18, Septuagint-transaltion)

To place trust or hope "in falsehood" is a bad policy, both for "rulers of people" in their governing, and for each of us in our personal lives. And by "falsehood" I mean various kinds of wishful thinking, about myself or others. This includes pretending to be who I am not, because of people-pleasing and fear, and imagining or expecting from others to be who/what they are not, according to my self-will alone. A "rushing storm," if it happens to come upon us, will bring down this house of cards.

I cannot "see" the truth about anything, actually, outside God and His light, because in my own, limited head I tend to "miss the mark." As Christ reminds the Pharisees, *"If you were blind, you would have no sin; but now that you say, 'We see,' your sin remains."* (Jn 9: 41) So today I let Christ, the Word of God, be the "precious corner-stone" in the foundations of my "house," that I may be protected in His humbling light, and in my blindness. *"The stone which the builders rejected has become the head corner-stone. This is the Lord's doing, and it is marvellous in our eyes."* (Ps 117/118: 22-23)

Meal Plan (A): *Strict Fast Day with No Oil – on New Calendar*
Meal Plan (B): *Fast Day with Oil – for Older Calendar Afterfeast of Annunciation/ Synaxis of Archangel Gabriel 2021*

FRIDAY, 4th WEEK

SHARERS IN EVERLASTING LIFE

"Now the powers of heaven minister invisibly with us. For, behold, the King of Glory enters. Behold the mystical sacrifice, fully accomplished, is ushered in. Let us draw near in faith and love, that we may become sharers/partakers (μέτοχοι, причастники) *in everlasting life. Alleluia, alleluia, alleluia."* (Liturgy of the Presanctified Gifts, Great Entrance hymn)

This is the hymn we sing at the Lenten Liturgy of the Presanctified Gifts, when the "mystical sacrifice" of the Body and Blood of Christ, the already-consecrated Gifts (consecrated at the Divine Liturgy of the previous Sunday), are transferred in a solemn procession from the Prothesis-table to the Holy Table in the altar. Here the unity of "us" with "the powers of heaven," of the earthly and the heavenly, the temporal and everlasting, is stressed, just as it is in the Byzantine Divine Liturgy. Why? Because the Body of Christ brings all of creation together, the visible and invisible.

So let me "draw near," as I am invited to do, that I may be a "sharer" or "partaker" not just of "life and life only" (in the words of Bob Dylan), but of "everlasting life," which extends above and beyond my smallness and brokenness. I am invited to share in the Body of Christ, – consecrated, broken, and given for me. So let me share in His brokenness, that I may be restored to wholeness, visible and invisible. Amen!

Meal Plan (A): *Strict Fast Day with No Oil*
*NOTE: Just two more weeks until Palm Sunday and Great/Passion Week left! Today if you can make it, the beautiful Lenten Liturgy of Presanctified Gifts is celebrated (on both calendars).

SATURDAY, 4th WEEK (of the reposed)

ENDING THE DAY WITH A PSALM

"How beloved are your dwellings, O Lord of Hosts; my soul longs and faints for the courts of the Lord. My heart and my flesh have rejoiced in the living God. For the sparrow has found herself a house, and the turtledove a nest for herself where she may lay her young, even your altars, O Lord of Hosts, my King and my God. Blessed are they that dwell in your house; unto ages of ages shall they praise you."
(Ps 83: 1-5, Septuagint-translation)

Psalm 83 is the first of the three psalms chanted at the final service of the daily cycle, the Ninth Hour. It is usually chanted in monasteries at the end of the workday, in the early evening and right before Vespers, which begins the liturgical cycle of the next day (because the liturgical "day" begins in the evening). As one can see in the passage quoted above, Psalm 83 can help us, at the end of a workday, to "come home" into the "dwellings" and "courts" of the Lord of Hosts.

This is true also for those of us who do not "come home" into a church every evening, – nor even on a weekly basis anymore, now that many churches are closed because of the Coronavirus. The words of Psalm 83 can be helpful for me as my day draws to an end in the middle of a now rather-quiet Vienna, to retrieve my sense of belonging to the Lord's "house," and "dwelling" in it, in His presence in my heart. Today, on this third Saturday of Lent, let me carry a verse or two of this Psalm with me, even as "my soul longs and faints for the courts of the Lord," so I can use it, nonetheless, to "come home" to my King and my God at the end of my day: *"How beloved are your dwellings, O Lord of Hosts; my soul longs and faints for the courts of the Lord. My heart and my flesh have rejoiced in the living God."*

Meal Plan (B): *Fast Day with Oil*
*NOTE: In Russian Orthodox and some other churches, this is a Memorial Saturday, when the deceased are commemorated. In Greek Orthodox parishes, Lenten Saturdays are usually dedicated to chanting (a part of) the Akathist-hymn to the Theotokos

4th SUNDAY OF LENT (of John Climacus)

THE DEAF AND DUMB SPIRIT

"And when Jesus saw that a crowd came running together, he rebuked the unclean spirit, saying to it, 'You dumb and deaf spirit, I command you, come out of him, and never enter him again.' And after crying out and convulsing him terribly, it came out, and the boy was like a corpse; so that most of them said, 'He is dead.' But Jesus took him by the hand and lifted him up, and he arose. And when he had entered the house, his disciples asked him privately, 'Why could we not cast it out?' And he said to them, 'This kind cannot be driven out by anything but prayer and fasting.'" (Mk 9: 25-29)

A "deaf and dumb spirit" afflicts me when I am unable to say what I need to say, for example, at confession, and hear what I need to hear, in open-hearted teachability. This kind of spirit traps me in circles of self-isolation and self-justification, doing the same self-destructive thing over and over again. So it was for the boy healed by Jesus, as the boy's father testifies: The spirit, says the father, *"has often cast him into the fire and into the water, to destroy him…"* (Mk 9: 22)

This Lent, let me come before my Lord and have this spirit cast out "by prayer and fasting." And I don't mean my own prayer and fasting, because I can't cast out my own demons, even if I were the world-champion of prayer and fasting. I mean, the prayer and fasting of the Church in this wonderful season, which offers me healing and liberation from my demons, if only I am willing to come and be healed. So let me come and be healed, in heartfelt confession and teachability. Lord, lift me up, that I may rise, by the prayers of Your holy Church. Amen!

Meal Plan (B): *Fast Day with Oil*

5th Week of Lent
MONDAY, 5th WEEK

WHY "FEAR" GOD?

"In the fear of the Lord is strong confidence: and he leaves his children a support. The commandment of the Lord is a fountain of life; and it causes men to turn aside from the snare of death." (Prov 14: 26-27, Septuagint-translation)

"Fear" is a life-giving, God-given gift, essential for survival. It is an evolved capacity in the human being, so science tells us. But like other God-given gifts and drives, which I inherently have as a human being, fear becomes harmful to me when it is divorced from God; when it is not "of God" and takes on a life of its own. Inherent, human fear in a life not God-focused is crippling, existential anxiety in the face of the many uncertainties and ambivalences that are part-and-parcel of any human life.

"In the fear of the Lord," I am reminded as I begin the fifth week of Lent, "is strong confidence." I "fear" losing my connection with Him and focus on Him, the Source of love, wisdom, and forgiveness of my sins, and this "fear of the Lord" liberates me from merely-human fears, of financial insecurity, of human opinion, of loneliness, and so on. "I walk the line" He sets out before me today, in the situations, work, and relationships I am given in my particular vocation, or "commandment of the Lord." So let me do the next right thing today, according to His call, – that is, according to my immediate responsibilities. Let my vocation be what it is meant to be today, "a fountain of life," which causes me "to turn aside from the snare of death."

Meal Plan (A): *Strict Fast Day with No Oil*
*NOTE: This fifth week of Lent is liturgically-eventful, with the Great Canon of St. Andrew of Crete chanted on Wednesday evening; and the entire Akathist-hymn to the Theotokos on Friday evening.

For more on this action-packed week, tune in to the "Morning Coffee" audio-podcast at **patreon.com/sistervassa**.
And re-connect with fellow Healthy*Fast*ers, as we walk this almost-final part of the fast together!

TUESDAY, 5th WEEK

DOES THE THEOTOKOS "SAVE" US?

"Most Holy Theotokos, save us!" (Byzantine prayer)

What, exactly, are we asking for in this prayer? Are we calling for another human being, Mary, to "save" us, as only our One Saviour and Lord Jesus Christ can?

No. We are calling for the "Birth-Giver of God" in the flesh, the "Theo-tokos," in Her unique ministry of bringing Him into the world, to bring us His salvation. He willed it to "save" the world in His incarnation, coming to us through Her over 2,000 years ago. And we believe in Him as in One Who continues to come to us, to "come again" and again (καὶ πάλιν ἐρχόμενον, и паки грядущаго) as the incarnate Lord.

Thus when we say, "Most Holy Theo-tokos, save us!" – and not "Mary, save us!" – we are calling also upon His name, the name of "God" incarnate, Who has brought us His salvation not without Her. We thus embrace that great mystery, of the Incarnation, when we say this today, because that mystery continues to work its salvific consequences in His One Body that is the Church. "Most Holy Theotokos, save us!" I say today, embracing His coming as He does, not only spiritually, but also physically, into holy communion with us.

Meal Plan (A): *Strict Fast Day with No Oil*

WEDNESDAY, 5th WEEK

THE GREAT CANON OF ST. ANDREW

"Two men went up into the temple to pray, one a Pharisee and the other a tax collector. The Pharisee stood and prayed thus with himself, 'God, I thank you that I am not like other men, extortioners, unjust, adulterers, or even like this tax collector. I fast twice a week, I give tithes of all that I get.' But the tax collector, standing far off, would not even lift up his eyes to heaven, but beat his breast, saying, 'God, be merciful to me a sinner!'" (Lk 18: 10-13)

Tonight in our churches we will be hearing the very long, "Great" Canon of St. Andrew of Crete. It contains many, many words: beautiful lamentations, biblical references, theological insights, and so on. It can be hard for us, with our present-day short attention-spans, to "follow" every word of this Canon. But the refrain to the Canon, repeated throughout the service, is easy to follow: "Have mercy on me, O God, have mercy on me." It reminds me of the simple prayer of the tax-collector in the parable quoted above, which we read in our churches at the very beginning of the Lenten season.

Let me keep things simple today, and open my heart to God's mercy. I give up and surrender to Him, approaching Him with nothing, in my lack of understanding and everything else. Because God has, where I lack. *"Have mercy on me, O God, have mercy on me."*

Meal Plan (B): *Fast Day with Oil*
*NOTE: This Wednesday, wine and oil are allowed, because of the physical strength we need for this evening's long church-service of the Great Canon of St. Andrew of Crete. The Liturgy of Presanctified Gifts is celebrated in the morning.

THURSDAY, 5th WEEK

WALKING ON PATHS UNKNOWN

"The Lord God of hosts shall go forth, and crush the war: he shall stir up jealousy, and shall shout mightily against his enemies… '…I will bring the blind by a way that they knew not, and I will cause them to walk paths which they have not known: I will turn darkness into light for them, and crooked things into straight. These things I will do, and will not forsake them. But they are turned back: be you utterly ashamed that trust in graven images, who say to the molten images, You are our gods.'" (Is 42: 13, 16-17, Septuagint-translation)

I am often shocked, really, by the very "human" expressions of God's divine zeal for saving us, His people. "I will do these things," He promises, "and will not forsake" you: "I will turn darkness into light" for you, He says, "and crooked things into straight." He will also "bring the blind," like me, "by a way that they knew not," and "will cause them to walk paths which they have not known."

But I should not be shocked, really, by God's willingness to do all this for me. Because He has done it already, time and again, in my life. So today, if I face the "darkness" of some uncertainties in life, or "paths which I have not known," or "crooked things," – whether at work, in personal relationships, or elsewhere, – let me not be "turned back" to God's loving, zealous willingness to lead me through it, as He always has. Thy will be done with me today, O Lord, as it was yesterday. Amen!

Meal Plan (B): *Fast Day with Oil*
*NOTE: This Thursday, wine and oil are allowed, because of the physical strength we need to recover after last evening's long church-service of the Great Canon of St. Andrew of Crete. The Liturgy of Presanctified Gifts is also celebrated this Thursday, with fewer great prostrations than usual.

FRIDAY, 5th WEEK

REMEMBERING DEATH

"My soul, my soul, arise! Why are you sleeping? The end is drawing near, and you will be confounded. Awake, then, and be watchful, that Christ our God may spare you, Who is everywhere present and fills all things." (Kontakion-hymn, Great Canon of St. Andrew)

Whether we like it or not, our mortality, or the fact that we will all, indeed, die a physical death, is something with which we are confronted more and more as we age. This fact really begins to "hit home" for many of us when we lose a parent, or notice our parents ageing. Psychologists observe that such reminders of our own mortality often cause depression, existential angst, and various unhealthy behaviours in middle-aged people in our time.

But there is nothing morbid or dark in "remembering death," as we are taught to do regularly in our beautiful Tradition. Here's the paradoxical thing about actively remembering death: It makes me more "watchful" and "awake" to life. I learn to pay attention more, to the presence of God in my here and now, in the people, places, and situations I am given today from Him, "Who is everywhere present and fills all things." I learn not to miss out on what I am called to do in the today, in usefulness to myself and others, rather than let life pass by and just "happen," as John Lennon said, "when you're not paying attention."

Let me "awake, then, and be watchful," on this sunny Friday. *"I shall not die, but live, and I shall tell of the works of the Lord."* (Ps 117/118: 17)

Meal Plan (A*): *Fast Day with Wine (but no oil)*
*NOTE: This Friday has an unusual fasting-rule, with wine but no oil allowed, because of this evening's joyous-but-physically-rigorous celebration of the Akathist-hymn to the Mother of God (a-kathist means "not seated," because one is supposed to stand, not sit, through the whole service). The Liturgy of Presanctified Gifts is also celebrated in the morning. Don't miss the Akathist-hymn!

SATURDAY, 5th WEEK (of the akathist hymn)

CAN'T START A FIRE WITHOUT A SPARK

"...And Mary said to the angel, 'How shall this be, since I have no husband?' And the angel said to her, 'The Holy Spirit will come upon you, and the power of the Most High will overshadow you; therefore the child to be born will be called holy, the Son of God. And behold, your kinswoman Elizabeth in her old age has also conceived a son; and this is the sixth month with her who was called barren. For with God nothing will be impossible.' And Mary said, 'Behold, I am the handmaid of the Lord; let it be to me according to your word.' And the angel departed from her.'" (Lk 1: 34-37)

The oft-unsung hero of this story, I think, is the Holy Spirit. It is He Who enables a teen-aged virgin from Nazareth, despite Mary's questions and confusion in the face of the strange news of the archangel, to conceive and give birth to the eternal Word of God in this world.

Now, please forgive me for some unconventional thoughts on this central moment in Salvation History. But it reminds me in general of our human, creative process. It is impossible to conceive, and give birth to, anything good in this world, I think, without that "spark" of the Holy Spirit. As Bruce Springsteen notes in his profound song about his own writing-process (Dancing in the Dark): "I ain't nothing but tired," he says, "Man I'm just tired and bored with myself / ...I could use just a little help / You can't start a fire without a spark..."

As we praise and magnify the Most-Holy Theotokos today, on this wonderful Saturday of the Akathist, let me embrace the Holy Virgin's openness to, and faith in, the Holy Spirit, with Whom "nothing will be impossible." I re-connect with Him today, in heartfelt prayer, as I approach my weekend-responsibilities, rather than isolate myself from God's creative energies in self-reliance, being "bored with myself." *"Behold, I am the handmaiden of the Lord; let it be to me according to your word."* Amen!

Meal Plan (B): *Fast Day with Oil*
*NOTE: The Divine Liturgy of St. John Chrysostom is celebrated today, as on all Saturdays of Lent, and we get some rest, enjoy a Weekend Treat, as we refresh our energies before entering the 6th week – the one leading up to Lazarus Saturday and Palm Sunday!

5th SUNDAY OF LENT (of St. Mary of Eygpt)

FORGIVEN FOR LOVE

"...Then turning toward the woman he (Jesus) said to Simon (the Pharisee), 'Do you see this woman? I entered your house, you gave me no water for my feet, but she has wet my feet with her tears and wiped them with her hair. You gave me no kiss, but from the time I came in she has not ceased to kiss my feet. You did not anoint my head with oil, but she has anointed my feet with ointment. Therefore I tell you, her sins, which are many, are forgiven, for she loved much; but he who is forgiven little, loves little.'" (Lk 7: 44-47)

This sinful woman "loved much," says the Lord. But who is it that this woman "loved much"? It is interesting to me that our Lord does not specify. It is clear from her actions that she loved our Lord "much." But He says about her, generally, that she "loved much." Because, I suspect, she generally "loved much," and gave of herself wholeheartedly, often irrationally, to others. She did this in love, – with all that love entails, like forgiving other sinners, perhaps her many lovers, who may have "trespassed against" her all the time, in her sinful life. This "loving much," as awkward as it was in the life of this woman, does not go unnoticed by the One Who knows our hearts. He gives her a break and says to her, *"Your sins are forgiven,"* and *"Your faith has saved you; go in peace."* (Lk 7: 48, 50)

This passage is a great consolation for those of us who have "loved much," even "too" much, and perhaps irrationally, making spectacles of ourselves, in love, as does this woman in the house of Simon the Pharisee. We can and do turn to the Lord of our hearts, with our tears, and are forgiven, even before we can forgive ourselves. *"O Lord, I have cried unto You. Hear me!"* (Ps 140/141: 1)

Meal Plan (B): *Fast Day with Oil*
*NOTE: The Divine Liturgy of St. Basil the Great is celebrated today, as on almost-all Sundays of Lent (except Palm Sunday). We get some rest and enjoy a Weekend Treat, as we refresh our energies before entering the 6th week – the one leading up to Lazarus Saturday and Palm Sunday!

6th Week of Lent
MONDAY, 6th WEEK

CALLED TO BE OURSELVES

"For many are called (κλητοὶ), *but few are chosen."* (Mt 22: 14)

A "calling" or "vocation" is common to all members of the "church" or "ekklesia" (from the Greek verb "ekkaleo," which means "to call out"). We are all "called" "according to his purpose" (Rom 8: 28) for each of us, according to our specific, God-given gifts and character. But it is not easy to discern God's voice in our lives (our specific "calling"), because we are burdened with other voices. They pull us away from being ourselves, the "selves" God wants us to be, and into a mainstream of popular masks behind which most of us feel safe.

A "vocation," as Karl Jung defines it, is "an irrational factor that destines a man to emancipate himself from the herd and from its well-worn paths." That is to say, it is liberating. But Jung also notes that "vocation" is "at once a charisma and a curse, because its first fruit is the conscious and unavoidable segregation of the single individual from the undifferentiated and unconscious herd. That means isolation…"

Let me ask God for courage today, to be myself, as He made me and sees me, that I may be liberated from wearing masks or trying to be someone else. Let me choose His voice today, that I may be "chosen" and liberated by Him, to be my "self" as He has envisioned it.

Meal Plan (A): Strict Fast Day with No Oil
*NOTE: The services of this sixth week of Lent, leading up to Lazarus Saturday, thematize the upcoming celebration of the Raising of Lazarus from the dead.

For more on the services of this week, tune in to the "Morning Coffee" audio podcast at **patreon.com/sistervassa**.
And re-connect with fellow Healthy*Fast*ers, as we walk this final stretch of the 40 Days together!

TUESDAY, 6th WEEK

I AM THE DOOR

"I am the door; if any one enters by me, he will be saved, and will go in and out and find pasture. The thief comes only to steal and kill and destroy; I came that they may have life, and have it abundantly. I am the good shepherd. The good shepherd lays down his life for the sheep. He who is a hireling and not a shepherd, whose own the sheep are not, sees the wolf coming and leaves the sheep and flees; and the wolf snatches them and scatters them. He flees because he is a hireling and cares nothing for the sheep. I am the good shepherd; I know my own and my own know me, as the Father knows me and I know the Father; and I lay down my life for the sheep. And I have other sheep, that are not of this fold; I must bring them also, and they will heed my voice. So there shall be one flock, one shepherd." (Jn 10:9-16)

We all need to "belong." Why? Because we were made that way, to share in, and be part of, God's Oneness and God's "abundant" Life. It is both spiritually and psychologically tormenting for us, to feel shut out from Life, like puzzle-pieces that just don't fit anywhere. Many people go through life feeling that way, or have felt that way, at some time or another.

Christ, the One Shepherd, is the "door" through Whom we, who were once outsiders and misfits, "enter" true Life, and become proper citizens of God's world. Other, merely-human community-builders might offer us some sense of belonging, – like the high priests of the Internet, or our political party, or clan, or some social circle, etc. But none of these "hirelings" can "save" us, that is to say, make us "whole" within ourselves and with God's world. Outside communion with Christ, we will find ourselves "scattered," at the end of the day. Thank You, Lord, for laying Your life down for us, and claiming us as Your own, and nobody else's. This Tuesday I hear Your voice, and take Your door, embracing the positive change with which you challenge me in this Lenten season, when you say: *"Repent!* (*Metanoeite!* – in Greek, meaning "Change your mind/your focus!") *For the kingdom of heaven is at hand."* (Mt 4: 17)

Meal Plan (A): *Strict Fast Day with No Oil*

WEDNESDAY, 6th WEEK

THE HOPE OF THE RESURRECTION

"Almighty Lord, You have created all things in wisdom. In Your inexpressible providence and great goodness You have brought us to these saving days, for the cleansing of our souls and bodies, for control of our passions, in the hope of the Resurrection. After the forty days You delivered into the hands of Your servant Moses the tablets of the law in characters divinely traced. Enable us also, O benevolent One, to fight the good fight, to complete the course of the fast, to keep the faith inviolate, to crush underfoot the heads of unseen tempters, to emerge victors over sin and to come, without reproach, to the worship of Your Holy Resurrection. For blessed and glorified is Your most honorable and majestic name…" (Lenten Liturgy of Presanctified Gifts, Opisthambonos-Prayer)

The "forty days" of Lent will end this Friday, because the upcoming days of Holy/Great Week (Страстная неделя) do not "count" as part of the forty, standing in a class of their own. Just a fun fact, in case you didn't know.

As the end of the forty days draws near, I'm particularly encouraged by one phrase in the above-quoted prayer: "the hope of the Resurrection." This hope is what keeps us going, – not only through Lent, but also through our cross-carrying journeys in general. It is not a hope that remains entirely unfulfilled in our earthly lives. As St. Gregory Palamas teaches us, we experience "a foretaste of the bodily resurrection" as we participate in the divine energies of God's grace in the here and now.

His grace is abundantly on offer today, not blocked off from me. So let me open up to Him in simple, heartfelt prayer, as Pascha draws near. O Lord, enable us also *"to come, without reproach, to the worship of Your Holy Resurrection."* Amen!

Meal Plan (A): *Strict Fast Day with No Oil*
*NOTE: The Liturgy of Presanctified Gifts is celebrated today. Enjoy a Midweek Treat, and let's stay focused as we prepare to greet the Lord as He comes to Bethany, and then enters Jerusalem – this upcoming Sunday!

THURSDAY, 6th WEEK

CHRISTS FINAL WORD

"Now a certain man was ill, Lazarus of Bethany, the village of Mary and her sister Martha... So the sisters (of Lazarus) sent to him, saying, 'Lord, he whom you love is ill.' But when Jesus heard it he said, 'This illness is not unto death; it is for the glory of God, so that the Son of God may be glorified by means of it.' Now Jesus loved Martha and her sister and Lazarus. So when he heard that he was ill, he stayed two days longer in the place where he was." (Jn 11: 1, 3-5)

Jesus "loved" Lazarus and his two sisters, these simple people, not extolled for any special virtue in the Gospels. Just as He loves all of us, for whom He died on the Cross "while we were still sinners" (Rom 5: 8). But when our Lord heard about Lazarus's deadly illness, which was so dire that Martha and Mary sent Him word of it, He "stayed two days longer in the place" where He was, not rushing over to Bethany to heal His good friend. The Son of God knew that Lazarus would die from this illness, but that his illness would, nonetheless, not be "unto death." Because death would not have "the final word" concerning Lazarus. The "final word" was that of the life-giving Word of God, Jesus Christ, Who was to raise His beloved friend from the dead several days later, saying, "Lazarus, come out!"

Nor does death have "the final word" concerning all of us, in the love of Christ. Because Christ has embraced us all, with His hands outstretched in His own "illness" on the Cross. But Christ's suffering was "not unto death," just as Lazarus's wasn't, even though both Christ and Lazarus truly died a physical death. And so are our illnesses and suffering "not unto death," when we embrace His word, in love. Even "while we are still sinners," in our imperfections.

So let me look death in the face today, and recognize that it no longer has "the final word" in my life. It has been vanquished by the love and friendship of my Lord Jesus Christ, Who grants me His life-giving word, making me capable of the Resurrection of Life. O Lord, may Your word be my "final word" today, that my "illness" not be unto death, even in my imperfections. Amen!

Meal Plan (A): *Strict Fast Day with No Oil*

FRIDAY, 6th WEEK

TRANSITIONING TO HOLY WEEK

"We have finished the spiritually-beneficial forty days! O Lover of Mankind, we ask: Grant us also to see the Holy Week of Your passion, that we may glorify Your mighty deeds, and Your ineffable dispensation for our sakes, as we sing with one mind: Lord, glory to You!" (Lenten Triodion, Friday of Week 6)

At this time, we are transitioning to the beginning of Holy Week, having "finished the forty days" of Lent, according to the count of the Byzantine liturgical calendar. Today Lazarus rests in his tomb for the third day, to be raised from the dead tomorrow by the all-powerful Word of God.

As I am carried into all these mysteries, which unfold before me in our beautiful traditions, I ask in the above-quoted hymn that I be given "to see" the great, "ineffable dispensation for our sakes." Indeed, I need to ask for this vision, lest the hustle-and-bustle of my pre-Paschal preparations distracts me from the Vanquisher of Death, Whom we now prepare to accompany into Jerusalem. Hosanna! Blessed is He Who comes in the name of the Lord!

Meal Plan (A): *Strict Fast Day with No Oil*
*NOTE: Some preparations are in order, as we approach Great Week! We might want to go to confession, so we might journal to prepare for that; We prepare palm-or pussywillow-branches (if we bring our own to church this Sunday); We buy some fish, as it's allowed on Palm Sunday, and maybe we begin baking our Paschal breads, do some spring-cleaning, etc., so we don't have all that to do in the final days preceding the Feast of Feasts. Congratulations on completing the 40 Days!

SATURDAY, 6th WEEK (Resurrection of Lazarus)

THE RESURRECTION OF LAZARUS

"Then Jesus, again greatly disturbed, came to the tomb. It was a cave, and a stone was lying against it. Jesus said, 'Take away the stone.' Martha, the sister of the dead man, said to him, 'Lord, already there is a stench because he has been dead four days.' Jesus said to her, 'Did I not tell you that if you believed, you would see the glory of God?' So they took away the stone. And Jesus looked upward and said, 'Father, I thank you for having heard me. I knew that you always hear me, but I have said this for the sake of the crowd standing here, so that they may believe that you sent me.' When he had said this, he cried with a loud voice, 'Lazarus, come out!' The dead man came out, his hands and feet bound with strips of cloth, and his face wrapped in a cloth. Jesus said to them, 'Unbind him, and let him go.'" (Jn 11: 38-44)

The resurrection of Lazarus is similar, in some ways, to the resurrection of our Lord Jesus Christ. There was "a cave, and a stone," and a "dead man came out…"

But Lazarus's resurrection was also quite different from our Lord's resurrection, which happened in silence. Lazarus was given new life through the spoken Word of God: Our Lord said, "Take away the stone," and prayed to the Father. And finally, He cried with a loud voice, "Lazarus, come out!"

But none of these words needed to be spoken, in the case of the glorious Resurrection of the eternal Word of God, our Lord Jesus Christ. Because in the case of the God-Man, the very Source of Life was, indeed, dead in "a cave," and sealed with "a stone," – but death "could not hold Him" (Acts 2: 24). His very divine essence, as Giver of Life and Vanquisher of Death, overcomes death, – in silence. His own, divine essence "speaks" for Him, overcoming death.

So let me depend on Christ's all-powerful, life-giving word a little bit more today, as we enter this Holy and Great Week of His passion and resurrection. He can, and does, "take away the stone" from my heart, regardless of the long-standing "stench" or other obstacles I've accumulated in my less-than-perfect Lent. O Lord, "unbind" me, and let me go, toward the upcoming Holy Week and Pascha. Amen!

Meal Plan (B**): *Fast Day with Oil - and Caviar!*
*NOTE: The unusual fasting-rule for Lazarus Saturday is that caviar is allowed, in addition to oil and wine. The Liturgy of St. John Chrysostom is celebrated, and this evening (or tomorrow morning) palm-branches are blessed and distributed at the matins-service of Palm Sunday.

PALM SUNDAY

THE LORD'S ENTRY INTO JERUSALEM

"The next day a great crowd who had come to the feast heard that Jesus was coming to Jerusalem. So they took branches of palm trees and went out to meet him, crying, 'Hosanna! Blessed is he who comes in the name of the Lord, even the King of Israel!' And Jesus found a young donkey and sat upon it; as it is written, 'Fear not, daughter of Zion; behold, your king is coming, sitting on an donkey's colt!' His disciples did not understand this at first; but when Jesus was glorified, then they remembered that this had been written of him and had been done to him. The crowd that had been with him when he called Lazarus out of the tomb and raised him from the dead bore witness. The reason why the crowd went to meet him was that they heard he had done this sign." (Jn 12: 12-18)

Today we similarly carry branches, "re-presenting," or "again making present" to ourselves and to our world, this historical event. Differently, however, from the great crowd in Jerusalem 2,000 years ago (and even Christ's disciples), we understand that we are not greeting an earthly king. Nor do we exclaim, "Hosanna! (Save, we pray!)," expecting from Him deliverance from our earthly or political foes. We greet the Vanquisher of Death, Who today enters Jerusalem to meet His death. And it is "by death," – by walking through it, – that He will "trample death." This victory will be invisible, very early next Sunday morning.

As we greet our Lord today, carrying branches as "signs of victory" (τῆς νίκης σύμβολα φέροντες, победы знамения носяще), I am reminded to "Fear not, daughter of Zion!" I'm reminded to "fear not" the journey of the Cross, which Christ has come to share with us, and to crown with His kind of victory, not ours. Let me "come" today, in His name, and be blessed. *"Blessed is he who comes in the name of the Lord!"*

Meal Plan (C): *Fast Day with Fish*

Holy and Great Week
HOLY & GREAT MONDAY

BEHOLD, THE BRIDEGROOM

"Behold, the Bridegroom comes at midnight, / And blessed is that servant whom He shall find watching, / And again, unworthy is the servant whom He shall find heedless. / Beware, therefore, O my soul, do not be weighed down with sleep, / Lest you be given up to death, and lest you be shut out of the Kingdom. / But rouse yourself crying: Holy, Holy, Holy, art Thou, O our God, / Through the Theotokos have mercy on us." (Troparion-Hymn of "Bridegroom Matins" on Holy Monday, Tuesday, and Wednesday)

This hymn, chanted in our churches at the morning-service of the first three days of this Holy and Great Week of our Lord's passion, refers to the Parable of the Ten Virgins (Mt 25: 1-13). In that well-known parable, there are five "wise" virgins, signifying those of us who are well-prepared, with "oil" in our "lamps," or with God's mercy and compassion in our hearts, when our "Bridegroom," Jesus Christ, arrives to invite us "in" to His feast. There are also five "foolish" virgins, who, like me, are not thus prepared.

So Jesus is the intended "Bridegroom" of all of us, – of the Church. Because what He seeks with each of us is union, or, more specifically, "communion." As St. Paul says about the marital union, *"This is a great mystery, and I am talking about Christ and His Church"* (Eph 5: 32).

Even if I've been "foolish" thus far, let me not be discouraged. Let me be "roused" at this point, opening my heart to God's mercy and compassion, as I am called in this beautiful hymn. My Bridegroom "comes" at the end of this week "at midnight," on the night of His glorious Resurrection, when we will be greeting Him, singing, "Christ is risen from the dead..." As I prepare for Pascha, I depend not on my own prayers or virtues for my "oil," but appeal to one Virgin wiser and more compassionate than all other "wise" virgins, the Mother of God: *"Through the Theotokos have mercy on us."*

Meal Plan (A): *Strict Fast Day with No Oil*
*NOTE: The Liturgy of Presanctified Gifts is celebrated this Monday, Tuesday, and Wednesday, for the final three times this year. And also – the beautiful "Bridegroom Matins," which you don't want to miss!

> For more on the services of this Holy and Great Week, join us for the "Morning Coffee" audio-podcast at **patreon.com/sistervassa**.
> And re-connect with fellow Healthy*Fast*ers, as we accompany the Lord in these final days before His passion.

HOLY & GREAT TUESDAY

I HAVE NO GARMENT

"I see Your bridal chamber adorned, O my Saviour, and I have not the garment, to enter therein; O Giver of Light, make radiant the vesture of my soul, and save me." (Exaposteilarion-Hymn of "Bridegroom Matins" on Holy Monday, Tuesday, and Wednesday)

Some of us have not fasted enough, or prayed enough, to be well-prepared for the upcoming celebration of Pascha. But in fact the hymns of this Holy and Great Week, like the one quoted above, speak of and for all of us, as ill-prepared for the "bridal chamber" that is the upcoming celebration. – Like the man in the Parable of the Wedding Banquet, who is found to have no "wedding garment," and is thrown out for his impropriety (Mt 22: 1-14).

But today let me let go of any preoccupation with my "ill-preparedness" and join the celebration, handing over "the vesture of my soul" to the Giver of Light. Because I have a Bridegroom Who has overcome my sinful state of affairs by taking them on, having been stripped naked, crucified, and vanquishing all that in His death and resurrection. O Lord, as You head toward Your cross for my sake, please do for me what I can't do for myself: **"Make radiant the vesture of my soul, and save me."**

Meal Plan (A): *Strict Fast Day with No Oil*
*NOTE: The Liturgy of Presanctified Gifts is celebrated this Tuesday, for the penultimate time this year. And also – the beautiful "Bridegroom Matins," which you don't want to miss!

For more on the services of this Holy and Great Week, join us for the "Morning Coffee" audio-podcast at **patreon.com/sistervassa**.
And re-connect with fellow Healthy*Fast*ers, as we accompany the Lord in these final days before His passion.

HOLY & GREAT WEDNESDAY

JUDAS THE "SCROOGE"

"Now when Jesus was at Bethany in the house of Simon the leper, a woman came up to him with an alabaster flask of very expensive ointment, and she poured it on his head, as he sat at table. But when the disciples saw it, they were indignant, saying, 'Why this waste? For this ointment might have been sold for a large sum, and given to the poor.' But Jesus, aware of this, said to them, 'Why do you trouble the woman? For she has done a beautiful thing for me (εἰς ἐμέ). For you always have the poor with you, but you will not always have me. In pouring this ointment on my body she has done it to prepare me for burial. Truly, I say to you, wherever this gospel is preached in the whole world, what she has done will be told in memory of her.' Then one of the twelve, who was called Judas Iscariot, went to the chief priests and said, 'What will you give me if I deliver him to you?' And they paid him thirty pieces of silver. And from that moment he sought an opportunity to betray him." (Mt 26: 6- 16)

So the woman who anoints Christ does "a beautiful thing" for Him, – personally and concretely for Jesus Christ, in the here and now. And that "here and now" happens to be this week of His passion, when he finds Himself on the outskirts of Jerusalem – a dangerous place because of the chief-priests who, at this point, were seeking to destroy Him. But the concern of "the disciples," which, according to another Gospel (Jn 12: 4-5) is voiced by Judas, is impersonal, – for "the (nameless) poor," in their unnamed needs in the uncertain future.

Judas is a miser, which means he views money as something to be hoarded for some future, vaguely-identified, need or calamity. It also means he has replaced with money the love and nourishment of a connection with others, including God, like Dickens's "Scrooge." Judas is "nurtured" by possessing money, having become dead to any real connection with Christ or anyone else. So, he acts alone, and he dies alone, with his "thirty pieces of silver" proving useless to him in the end.

Let me keep watch today, on this Holy and Great Wednesday, that any money I may possess is not, delusionally, "a beautiful thing" for me. A truly "beautiful thing" is to do, with money, what I am called to do in the here and now, according to my vocation. And that means, doing for those in my here and now, whom I have been called to serve and minister to, according to my concrete responsibilities and God-given relationships. For I will always have "the poor" with me, but I may not always have these beloved people in my vicinity.

Meal Plan (A): *Strict Fast Day with No Oil*
*NOTE: The Liturgy of Presanctified Gifts is celebrated this Wednesday, for the last time this year. And also – the beautiful "Bridegroom Matins," which you don't want to miss!

HOLY & GREAT THURSDAY

A NEW COVENANT

"And when the hour came, he sat at table, and the apostles with him. And he said to them, 'I have earnestly desired to eat this passover with you before I suffer; for I tell you I shall not eat it until it is fulfilled in the kingdom of God.' And he took a cup, and when he had given thanks he said, 'Take this, and divide it among yourselves; for I tell you that from now on I shall not drink of the fruit of the vine until the kingdom of God comes.' And he took bread, and when he had given thanks he broke it and gave it to them, saying, 'This is my body which is given for you. Do this in remembrance of me.' And likewise the cup after supper, saying, 'This cup which is poured out for you is the new covenant in my blood. But behold the hand of him who betrays me is with me on the table.'" (Lk 22: 14-20)

"Take this," Jesus says, on this Holy and Great Thursday, "and divide it among yourselves." Because He is, shockingly, entrusting the distribution of His "new covenant," of sacramental communion with His goodness and God-ness, in Body and Blood, to His imperfect followers, the Apostles. – Most of these men, except John, were about to abandon Him at the time of His arrest and crucifixion, in case you didn't know.

But all that, – all of our human weakness, was overcome and made OK, by our Lord's death and resurrection, because He "trampled" our human darkness and death, by walking through it Himself. Our "new covenant" or "new connection" with God and all His goodness is, simply put, Him. In the flesh. In His Body and Blood. He does for us what we never could do for ourselves. I can "do" in Him and with Him what I could never do in and with my own self.

So let me let go of self-reliance and self-preoccupation today, and partake of Him, despite my imperfection. He gives of Himself to my imperfection, by the hands of His imperfect ministers, in this great sacrament He instituted today, of Holy Communion. It is not about us. As I "do this" it is not about me, but rather "in remembrance of Him," lest I forget Who it is, Who accomplishes my salvific, new connection, or "new covenant," with God and all his good creation. So let me communicate today, in and with Him, rather than self-isolate. *"Of Your mystical Supper, O Son of God, accept me today as a communicant!"* (Вечери твоея тайныя днесь, Сыне Божий, причастника мя приими…)

Meal Plan (B): *Fast Day with Oil*
*NOTE: The Divine Liturgy of St. Basil is celebrated on this Holy and Great Thursday, and oil & wine are allowed, ahead of the strict-fasting tomorrow. We try to get to church today and receive Holy Communion, if at all possible!

HOLY & GREAT FRIDUSAY

MY GOD, MY GOD, WHY...?

"And when the sixth hour had come, there was darkness over the whole land until the ninth hour. And at the ninth hour Jesus cried with a loud voice, 'Elo-i, Elo-i, lama sabachthani?' which means, 'My God, my God, why have you forsaken me?' And some of the bystanders hearing it said, 'Behold, he is calling Elijah.' And one ran and, filling a sponge full of vinegar, put it on a reed and gave it to him to drink, saying, 'Wait, let us see whether Elijah will come to take him down.' And Jesus uttered a loud cry, and breathed his last. And the curtain of the temple was torn in two, from top to bottom. And when the centurion, who stood facing him, saw that he thus breathed his last, he said, 'Truly this man was the Son of God!'" (Mk 15: 33-39)

Centuries before the events of this Holy and Great Friday, when the All-powerful became powerless, and the Life-Giver died, the Prophet Isaiah explained that "we" were the ones "in trouble," and not Him, even while those who had Him crucified believed He was disrupting "our peace." But He took our "trouble" and false "peace" upon Himself, in order to expose it, and vanquish it, in Him: *"He bears our sins,"* Isaiah proclaims, *"and is pained for us: yet we accounted him to be in trouble, and in suffering, and in affliction. But he was wounded on account of our sins, and was bruised because of our iniquities: the chastisement of our peace* (παιδεία εἰρήνης ἡμῶν) *was upon him; and by his wounds we were healed."* (Is 53: 4- 5)

As I weep today, with the Church, beholding the crucifixion, abandonment, and death of our Lord many Fridays ago, I remember that He takes all our darkness upon Himself wilfully, in order to bring us out of it into new Life and new Light, with Him and in Him. He takes on our derision, anger, cruelty, despair, and injustice, – so we no longer need to unleash those things on one another, nor upon ourselves. "For God so loved the world." (Jn 3: 16) Glory be to Him.

Meal Plan (A***): *Strict Fast Day with no Oil*
*NOTE: On this Holy and Great Friday, we fast entirely, if possible, from all food, until Vespers, at which the Epitaphios (Плащаница) is brought out. If one must eat, consider a light salad with some boiled potatoes after this service. (This was the tradition in my parents home when I was growing up.) And we try to observe silence, abstain from social media, etc.

HOLY & GREAT SATURDAY

THE SILENCE OF HOLY SATURDAY

"When You did descend to death, O Life Immortal, / You did slay hell with the splendor of Your Godhead, / And when from the depths You did raise the dead, / All the Powers of Heaven cried out, / O Giver of Life, Christ our God, glory to You!" (Troparion-hymn of Holy & Great Saturday)

The great "silence" of Holy Saturday, when the God-Man lies in the tomb, is different for all those involved. For Joseph of Arimathea and the women who had seen "how his body was laid," and now, on the Sabbath, "rested according to the commandment" (Lk 23: 56), it was a day of great mourning and buried hope.

For us, however, today's "silence" is more like the calm before a storm. Because we know that the Lord of the Sabbath is "working" even as "all mortal flesh" is silent in the face of His horrifying death: *"My Father is working still,"* He told us on another Saturday, "and I am working." (Jn 5: 17)

And so it is on this Great and Holy Saturday, when the Source of Life descends into death and hell, not as one defeated, but as Victor; as One Whom "death could not hold." (Acts 2: 24) He "slays hell" already today, and brings new life, in Him, to those who were stuck there. This is why our icon of the feast of the Resurrection depicts this day, Holy Saturday, or Christ's victorious descent into Hades. *"O Giver of Life,"* as we anticipate Your exit from the Tomb in the great silence of today, *"Christ our God, glory to You!"*

Meal Plan (A*): *__Strict Fast Day with no Oil, but Wine is Allowed__*
*On this Holy and Great Saturday, on which we observe a silence of a different kind (from Holy Friday), of excited anticipation of the Lord's exit from the Tomb, we don't want to miss the morning Divine Liturgy, at which we get a foretaste of the Paschal joy, coming up tonight at the Midnight Vigil! *Please see* **Meal Plan (F)** *for some tips on how to transition from fasting to feasting this upcoming night.*

PASCHA-SUNDAY (The Resurrection of Our Lord)

WHY DO YOU SEEK THE LIVING AMONG THE DEAD?

"But on the first day of the week, at early dawn, they came to the tomb, taking the spices that they had prepared. They found the stone rolled away from the tomb, but when they went in, they did not find the body. While they were perplexed about this, suddenly two men in dazzling clothes stood beside them. The women were terrified and bowed their faces to the ground, but the men said to them, 'Why do you seek the living among the dead? He is not here, but has risen...'" (Lk 24: 1-6)

The two angels, the "two men in dazzling clothes" are not all that direct in delivering the news of the resurrection. First, they allow the women to be "perplexed" for a bit, about the rolled-away stone. And then "suddenly," the two make their appearance, and introduce themselves with the silliest question: "Why do you seek the living among the dead?"

Now, please excuse me, – But what a question! I mean, after all that had happened, of COURSE these heartbroken women sought their crucified and buried Lord "among the dead." After all, they had seen Him breathe His last, and die, and be buried. And then they had spent all of Saturday in deep mourning.

But here's the charming thing about this vital moment in Salvation History: The two angels apparently take delight in delivering the good news of Christ's resurrection to the women in this playful, gradual way: "Why," they first ask, "do you seek the living among the dead?" Only after that, they deliver the good news, and explain: "He is not here, but is risen…"

I have no deep theological point to make here today, except to note the playfulness of our joy today, in our Lord's resurrection. Christ is risen from the dead, so let all the darkness and earnestness of death be trampled, by Him. Christ is risen, dear zillions! So please relax, and enjoy the grace of the feast!

Meal Plan (F): *Pascha! Transitioning from Fasting to Feasting*

Bright Week

BRIGHT MONDAY

HE KNOWS MY NAME

"But Mary stood weeping outside the tomb. As she wept, she bent over to look into the tomb; and she saw two angels in white, sitting where the body of Jesus had been lying, one at the head and the other at the feet. They said to her, 'Woman, why are you weeping?' She said to them, 'They have taken away my Lord, and I do not know where they have laid him.' When she had said this, she turned around and saw Jesus standing there, but she did not know that it was Jesus. Jesus said to her, 'Woman, why are you weeping? Whom are you looking for?' Supposing him to be the gardener, she said to him, 'Sir, if you have carried him away, tell me where you have laid him, and I will take him away.' Jesus said to her, 'Mary!' She turned and said to him in Hebrew, 'Rabbouni!' (which means Teacher)." (Jn 20: 11-16)

Mary Magdalene does not recognize our Lord, nor does she stop weeping, until He says her name: "Mary!" Because He said it like nobody else. In His divine love and omniscience, the Lord really "knew" her name; He knew, and understood, her entire identity, – what and who she was, and what and who she wasn't. So, she takes great consolation in hearing Him call her name.

Today I take great consolation in being "known," understood, and called, as all of us are, by our one-and-only Creator and Teacher. He does not torment me by "not understanding" me. So I can be myself, and let go of any masks I may wear for other, simply-human beings, as I approach Him today, in simple and heartfelt prayer.

"Woman, why are you weeping?" He asks me today, and "Whom are you looking for?" I can stop weeping, and stop looking, because my Teacher is alive and well today, for my sake. Christ is risen from the dead, dear zillions, "and cannot die again" (Rom 6: 9). So let me respond to Him, Who loves and knows me, as I am.

Meal Plan (E): *No Fasting Day*
NOTE*: After Lent, *more daily exercise* is recommended. That is to say, instead of the Lenten 20-30 minute daily brisk walk, treat yourself to a 40 min – 1 hour daily walk outside the fasting season!

BRIGHT TUESDAY

A NEW DRINK

"Come, let us drink a new drink (Δεῦτε πόμα πίωμεν καινόν, Приидите пиво пием новое), */ not one miraculously brought forth from a barren rock / but the Fountain of Incorruption, / springing forth from the tomb of Christ, // in Whom we are strengthened."* (Paschal Canon, Irmos of Ode 3)

The Lord's resurrection changes things, including our "drinking habits." That is to say, the new Life and new Strength "springing forth from the tomb" is offered to me as a new "Fountain," to which I can come and quench my inner "thirst," or the hole in my heart. It is not merely water "brought forth from a barren rock," as Moses did for his people in the water-less desert (Numbers 20: 11).

We "are strengthened" continuously, on a daily basis, in and through communion with Christ, Who walks with us on our cross-carrying journeys, as One already-victorious, as One Who knows well, and has overcome, the full extent of our darkness and difficulties. So today let me "come," once again, and "drink a new drink," offered to me in abundance in the Self-Offering of my Lord, Who is risen indeed!

Meal Plan (E): *No Fasting Day*
NOTE*: After Lent, *more daily exercise* is recommended. That is to say, instead of the Lenten 20-30 minute daily brisk walk, treat yourself to a 40 min – 1 hour daily walk in the springtime sunshine – or rain!

BRIGHT WEDNESDAY

HE COULDN'T BE HELD

"'Men of Israel, hear these words: Jesus of Nazareth, a man attested to you by God with mighty works and wonders and signs which God did through him in your midst, as you yourselves know— this Jesus, delivered up according to the definite plan and foreknowledge of God, you crucified and killed by the hands of lawless men. But God raised him up, having loosed the pangs of death, because it was not possible for him to be held by it.'" (St. Peter's speech on Pentecost, Acts 2: 22-24)

Pentecost is still many weeks away, but I am already called to anticipate it in the above-quoted passage, read in our churches today. Here St. Peter, filled with the Holy Spirit, is "making sense" of Christ's death and resurrection. He offers me the simplest and clearest "explanation" of our Lord's rising up from the dead, – "because it was not possible for Him to be held" by death. Divinity, the Source of Life, could not be held by death. Humanity, on the other hand, "could" be held by death, and was, indeed, "held" by it, – before humanity's unique union with divinity in the Person of Jesus Christ. When death came up against the God-Man, Who took it on wilfully, "according to the definite plan and foreknowledge of God," it was irreparably damaged, losing its "sting" and its "hold" on all who wilfully choose to live and die in Christ.

We still die a physical death, but we die differently, just like we live differently, in Christ. The meaning of "death" and "life" is forever changed through Christ's salvific journey through our life and our death. It is now His kind of death, and His kind of life, that we receive, if we wilfully walk the cross-carrying journey with Him. But just talking about it, or reading about it, doesn't do me much good. I need to try it today, and once again re-connect with His Spirit, that I may experience this new kind of living and dying, not in lonely isolation, but as one belonging to His light-filled Body. So that I know what it means, not to be "held" by death. Thank You, Lord, for being One of us, that we may become one, in You.

Meal Plan (E): *No Fasting Day*
NOTE*: To be super-annoying, here's another reminder that after Lent, *more daily exercise* is recommended! That is to say, instead of the Lenten 20-30 minute daily brisk walk, treat yourself to a 40 min – 1 hour daily walk in the springtime sunshine – or rain!

BRIGHT THURSDAY

SHINE, SHINE!

"Shine, shine (Φωτίζου, φωτίζου, Светися, светися), O New Jerusalem, for the glory of the Lord has risen upon you. Dance now and be glad, O Sion, and you rejoice, pure Mother of God, at the arising of Him to Whom you gave birth." (Paschal Canon, Irmos of Ode 9)

Here are some fun facts about this well-known hymn of our Paschal services. It begins by paraphrasing the words of Isaiah 60: 1, according to the Septuagint: "Shine, shine, O Jerusalem (Φωτίζου, φωτίζου, Ιερουσαλημ)," says Isaiah, "for your light is come, and the glory of the Lord is risen upon you." The hymn is referring these words to the "new" Jerusalem or Sion, – the Church, – in other words, all of us.

And finally the hymn addresses yet another image of the Church, the Mother of God. She classically signifies the Church, because the Church, i.e., each of us, is called to give birth to the Word of God in this world. So let me do so today, and let me "shine," as I am called to, with and in my risen Lord. Because "my light is come," as prophesied by Isaiah, and He is risen indeed!

Meal Plan (E): *No Fasting Day, with extra post-Lenten exercise!*

BRIGHT FRIDAY

THOSE IN THE TOMBS (СУЩИЕ ВО ГРОБЕХ)

"Christ is risen from the dead, / trampling down death by death, / and upon those in the tombs (καὶ τοῖς ἐν τοῖς μνήμασι, и сущим во гробех) / *bestowing life!"* (Byzantine Troparion-hamn of Pascha/Easter)

So – who are "those in the tombs"? All of us, practically. "Those in the tombs" are those of us "buried," either in our work or in a relationship, or in a "dead" indifference to work or a relationship (I realize that sounds paradoxical, but both those situations are "deadening"); or in some obsession or addiction, like an unhealthy dependency on a thing or person.

But Christ "is risen" from all our darkness, having walked through it; having confronted all our weakness, anger, resentment, fear, despondency, and insufficiency, which led Him to the Cross, – which was His calling or "vocation." He "trampled" all our "death" and deadness, by walking through that "death," and rising from it, as He was "called" to do by the Father, and as only He could, as the Source of Life, in His divinity.

So I can also walk through it all today, but not on my own. I can trample death "by death," by walking in and with Him through my vocation and responsibilities, which may, at times, – when I try to tackle them on my own, – seem dark and deadening. But, paradoxically, they (my vocation and responsibilities) are also the very thing that leads me to life, because I am called to do them. And Christ has paved the way for me, which is the way of the Cross, of not avoiding my responsibilities, but walking through them, in and with Him. So let me receive life, by walking through it, because it is "bestowed" to me by One Who knows the way out of my "tomb," which is, paradoxically, my vocation. So let me take it up today, handing it over to Him in heartfelt prayer, and opening up to His help. "Christ is risen from the dead," dear zillions, "trampling down death by death, and upon those in the tombs bestowing life!"

Meal Plan (E): *No Fasting Day*
NOTE*: *Don't forget your post-Lenten daily walk in the Paschal sunshine.* ☺

BRIGHT SATURDAY

THE BREAD OF LIFE

"Jesus said to them, 'I am the bread of life (ὁ ἄρτος τῆς ζωῆς); *he who comes to me shall not hunger, and he who believes in me shall never thirst. But I said to you that you have seen me and yet do not believe. All that the Father gives me will come to me; and him who comes to me I will not cast out..."* (Jn 6: 35-37)

Today, on Bright Saturday, the special Easter "Bread" or "Artos," which we see on a small table before the iconostasis in our churches all of Bright Week, is broken and distributed to the faithful. The "Artos" was first blessed on the night of Pascha, and carried around the church in processions throughout this week. It signifies, or points to, the presence of the Lord among us, His disciples, after His resurrection.

So that is why I'm thinking about this passage, in which Christ calls Himself "the bread of life." Here He also says to the crowd, nay, pleads with the crowd, to believe Him. "You have seen me and yet do not believe." Because He knows we are a disbelieving bunch, with "trust issues" when it comes to Him. Nonetheless, if you "come to me," however and whoever you are, He assures me, I will not cast you out.

And tomorrow, on Thomas Sunday, He will further address our doubts, and further assure us, also those of us who did not see Him in the flesh as those first disciples did: "Blessed are those who have not seen," He will say to all of us, "and yet have believed." (Jn 20: 29) So today "Do not be faithless, but believe" (Jn 20: 27), I hear Him say to me, because I have that choice. I can, indeed, approach Him, the Bread of Life, once again. And once again, I will not hunger, or thirst, or, indeed, be "cast out," for He is risen indeed!

Meal Plan (E): *No Fasting Day*

Christ is risen, dear HealthyFasters – and Healthy-Feasters!
Thank you for joining us on this journey, and please stay healthy.

Meal Plans

MEAL-PLANS (A), (B), (C), (D), (E), and (F), FOR VARIOUS TYPES OF FAST/FEAST-DAYS

in collaboration with Denise Canellos, MS, CNS
(an asterisk* means you can find the HealthyFast recipe in the final section of this Guidebook)

Meal Plan (A)
Strict Fast Day with No Oil

No meat, poultry, fish, dairy, oil, or wine (shellfish is allowed, but if you are watching your weight, limit it to your "Wednesday Treat," and to once or twice more over the Lenten weekends).
Note: Fasting from oil does not mean a no-fat diet. It is important to get our essential fatty acids, and on oil-free days we get those from foods such as nuts, seeds, and avocado.

(A)   Breakfast

Option 1: Oatmeal (1/2 cup / 57g uncooked)
Non-dairy milk of choice (unsweetened)
Fresh or frozen fruit of choice (at least 1/2 cup/ 85 - 115 g)
Nuts (1-2 ounces / 28-57 g / 1-2 handfuls)
If you are using dried fruit, try to select one without added sugar (1/4 cup or 43 g.)

Option 2: Whole grain toast (1-2 slices)
Sliced or mashed avocado (1/2 average-size fruit) or homemade tofu-spread (make it with 6oz / 170g soft/silk tofu, and seasoning of choice) with
Sesame or unshelled hemp seeds, furikake (a Japanese seasoning with sesame seeds and seaweed), or your topping of choice sprinkled on top
Fruit (1 piece or 1 cup/or handful of cut fruit/berries)
Small container of non-dairy yogurt (optional)

Option 3: Oil-Free Breakfast Skillet & Toast Ingredients:
- 1 cup/128g sliced mushrooms
- 1 cup/128g diced zucchini
- ½ cup/64g onion, red or white
- ½ cup/64g chopped green onion
- handful of chopped fresh cilantro
- ½ a red pepper, diced
- 9 oz/255g of black beans OR vegan-sausage OR tofu OR chickpeas
- 1 tsp each garlic powder and chili powder
- ½ tsp cumin and paprika OR cumin and turmeric

- salt & pepper, to taste
- ½ sliced avocado and ca. 1 Tbs salsa, for topping

Instructions: Cook everything (except avocado & salsa, obviously) in a preheated skillet/non-stick pan over medium-high heat, until the vegetables are soft and browned, about 6-7 minutes. Add water as needed, if it begins to stick. Season with salt & black pepper to taste. Top with avocado & salsa and extra chopped green onions, and enjoy with 1-2 slices of whole wheat toast.

(A) Lunch

Option 1: Grain, Protein & Vegetables; a fiber-rich cooked grain (quinoa/buckwheat/whole grain farro) is ¼ of your plate, a protein-rich food (tofu or beans/lentils/chickpeas/other legumes) is ¼ of your plate, and salad/cooked vegetables and/or fruit is ½ of your plate
TIP: Cook double the portion, and have the extra portion for dinner.

Option 2: Lentil and vegetable soup, made without oil*
Small side salad of greens and vegetables with 1-2 Tbs/15-30ml Oil-Free Creamy Vegan Dressing* (or made with Non-Dairy Yogurt & sugarless Dijon Mustard & seasoning to taste)
Whole grain roll on the side (optional) Piece of fruit or 1 cup/170-230g of cut fruit
TIP: Cook double the portion, and have the extra portion for dinner.

Option 3: Beans/Lentils/Chickpeas & Large salad; cooked/canned beans, lentils, or chickpeas are 1/3 of your plate, and salad (mixed greens, raw broccoli finely-chopped, radishes, celery, red onion, cucumbers, tomatoes), with 2-3 Tbs / 30-45 ml Oil-Free Creamy Vegan Dressing* is 2/3 of your plate
1 whole grain roll or 1-2 slices of whole grain bread

Option 4: Healthy Pasta & Tofu-Sauce: Cook 2 handfuls (dry) red-lentil penne. Sauce: Cut 1 average-size zucchini and 1-2 tomatoes in small pieces, crush 2-3 cloves garlic, and sautee in non-stick pan, adding water & vinegar as needed to avoid sticking, and salt & pepper to taste; Mash up ca. 6 oz / 170 g soft/ "silk" tofu (or make into sauce using hand-mixer) and season that with herbs & Dijon mustard, or turmeric/curcuma & black pepper, or sugar-free soy sauce & chives, add to zucchini, tomatoes & garlic and mix together. Serve over pasta and garnish with fresh parsley or chives.
Piece of fruit or 1 cup/170-230g of cut fruit

Option 5: Oil-Free Turmeric-Chickpea Salad Sandwich Ingredients:
- 1 15 oz/400g can chickpeas
- 1/3 cup/79ml Oil-Free Vegan Mayonnaise*
- ½ teaspoon turmeric (curcuma)
- ½ teaspoon onion powder
- 1 clove garlic, minced
- black pepper & salt to taste

Instructions: Drain the chickpeas and mix all ingredients with electric hand-mixer or in a blender, but not too mushy so you still have some texture! Enjoy on whole wheat bread.
Green salad (2 cups/50g greens with tomatoes and any other vegetables you like)
Oil-Free Vegan Dressing* (2 Tbs/30ml)
Piece of fruit or 1 cup/230g cut fruit / or handful of berries

(A) Dinner

Option 1: Grain, Protein & Vegetables or Soup (Left-Over From Lunch): a fiber-rich cooked grain (quinoa/buckwheat/whole grain farro) is 1/4 of your plate, a protein-rich food (tofu or beans/lentils/chickpeas/other legumes) is ¼ of your plate, and cooked vegetables are 1/2 of your plate OR have the Lentil & Vegetable Soup with an optional whole grain roll or 1-2 slices of whole grain bread on the side

Option 2: Tofu & Vegetable Stir Fry (stir-fry using apple cider vinegar & water OR oil-free vegetable broth; season with sugar-free soy sauce, fresh chives, or turmeric & black pepper & salt, and sprinkle with sesame seeds) - Tofu is 1/3 of your plate; Vegetables 2/3.

Option 3: Chickpea Curry (recipe for 2 portions)
Ingredients:
- 1 small red onion, chopped
- 1 clove garlic, minced
- 1 Tbs. curry powder
- 1 tsp. cumin powder
- 1 tsp. ground coriander
- 1 tsp. ground paprika
- 1 tsp. dried ginger
- 1 14-ounce / 397 g. can of diced tomatoes
- 1 14-ounce / 397 g. can of low-sodium or no-salt-added chickpeas (drained and rinsed)
- 1 ½ cups / 355 ml. unsweetened almond milk
- 2 Tbs. Maple syrup
- Salt and pepper to taste

Instructions: 1. Preheat a large, non-stick pan over medium heat; 2. While it's heating, mix curry powder, coriander, cumin, paprika, and ginger in a bowl; 3. Cook onions and garlic on preheated pan, adding 2 Tbs of water (cook until onions are soft); 4. Sprinkle the spice-mixture onto the garlic & onions, mixing until onions are covered, and add a bit of water if needed to prevent sticking; 5. Add chickpeas, tomatoes, and almond-milk to the pan and mix well; Bring to a simmer and cook for 2-3 minutes; 6. Reduce heat to medium-low, add maple-syrup, and season to taste with salt & pepper. 7. Serve with brown rice or baked/steamed vegetables (on 1/3 of your plate), or enjoy as a soup on its own!

Option 4 (Wednesday Treat): Shrimp/Other Seafood (7 – 9 oz. / 200 – 250 g), Healthy Pasta (ca. 2 handfuls dry) & Vegetables: Grill or steam the shrimp/scallops/calamari, and use whole-grain pasta or pasta made of lentils or beans, and mix the pasta with a handful of asparagus-tips or broccoli in a non-dairy yogurt sauce (2-3 Tbs, seasoned to taste with either: 1. Sugarless Dijon mustard & soy sauce; 2. lemon, garlic, and seasoned salt; or 3. Turmeric & black pepper & salt)

(A) Snack Options:
-Apple with natural peanut butter (1-2 Tbs/15-30g)
-Trail mix - raw nuts, seeds, and dried fruit (1/4 cup/43 g)
-Starbuck's Extra-Dry "Tall" (small) Cappucino with Oat, Soy, or Almond Milk
-Carrot- and celery-sticks with oil-free hummus, or Homemade Tofu Dip* (1/4 cup/43 g)
-Tofu-Mousse-Dessert* (w Apple & Cinnamon, or Berries, or Pineapple & Mint)
-Pickle with Oil-Free Vegan Mayonnaise* (1 Tbs)
-(Midweek & Weekend Treat Snacks):
-**Air-popped popcorn** (see below) with seasoning of choice (3 cups/24g popped)
-**Berries & Mint Shake** (7 oz/200g frozen Mixed Berries; 1 cup / 250ml Oat-Milk unsweetened; 2-3 ice-cubes and/or water; fresh mint-leaves; add 1-2 dashes of liquid Stevia if desired)
-**Papaya & Watermelon Smoothie** (50g papaya, 100g watermelon, 1 Tbs lemon-juice, 2-3 ice cubes, mixed in a blender)

Note about popcorn: air-popped uses only hot air to pop the kernels and is oil-free. Most microwave popcorn uses some oil for popping. If using, choose ones with the fewest additives, and ones that you know what all of the ingredients actually are. You can pop your own in the microwave without oil (just ad 1/3 cup kernels to a brown paper lunch bag, fold over the top and cook until the popping stops). Or pop in hot oil in the traditional way, if/when you are using oil.

Meal Plan (B)
Fast Day with Oil

*No meat, poultry, dairy, or fish (shellfish is allowed, but if you are watching your weight, limit it to your "Wednesday Treat," and to once or twice more over the Lenten weekends), plus oil and wine is allowed. This **(B)** fasting-rule applies to all weekends of Lent, – or to all days of Lent, if you (and your family) fast with oil.*
*For **(B)**-days you can use the meals in **(A)** made with oil, and:*

(B) Breakfast

Option 1: Oatmeal (1/2 cup / 57g uncooked) with 1 Tbs nut-butter of choice on top (try it!)
Non-dairy milk of choice (unsweetened)
Fresh or frozen fruit of choice (at least 1/2 cup/86g)
If you are using dried fruit, try to select one without added sugar (1/4 cup/ 43g)

Option 2: Whole grain toast (1-2 slices) with
Hummus-made-with-oil, or nut butter of choice (2 Tbs/30g), OR
Sliced/mashed avocado (1/2 average size fruit) with
Sesame, pumpkin, or un-shelled hemp seeds, or furikake (a Japanese seasoning with sesame seeds and seaweed) sprinkled on top
Fruit (1 piece or 1 cup/230g or handful of cut fruit/berries)
Small container of non-dairy yogurt (optional)

Option 3: Tofu Scramble & Toast Ingredients:
- 1 Tbs olive oil
- ¼ of an onion, diced
- 2 garlic cloves (chopped finely) or use powder
- 2-3 cups/256-384g chopped vegetables – use "saute-able" vegetables like asparagus, mushrooms, snow peas, bell pepper, carrots, shredded cabbage, zucchini, kale, carrots, chard, or whatever you have.
- 8 oz / 227g tofu, blotted with paper towels, and either cut into cubes, or crumbled
- salt & black pepper to taste
- ¼ to ½ tspn turmeric/curcuma (optional)
- small splash of sugar-free soy sauce (or "Bragg's liquid amino acid)
- additional toppings (all optional) – fresh herbs or sprouts, ½ sliced avocado, sunflower or un-shelled hemp or pumpkin seeds.
- 1-2 slices of whole wheat toast

Instructions: 1. Heat oil in a large skillet or non-stick pan. Sauté onion 2 minutes over medium high heat, then turn heat to medium & add garlic and other veggies. Lightly salt. Sauté until "al dente," turning heat down if necessary and/or covering. 2. Once veggies are just tender, make a hole in the center of the pan and add the tofu, and sauté it at medium heat. If the tofu sticks – instead of adding more oil- try letting it form a golden crust, before trying to flip it. (When something "browns" in a pan, it will naturally detach from the pan.) 3. Season the tofu with salt, black pepper and turmeric/curcuma. 4. When tofu is starting to have some crispy edges, mix it into the veggies, and taste. If it tastes bland, it most likely needs a little salt, and you might add a very tiny drizzle of sugarless soy sauce or of "Bragg's liquid aminos." (Use a light hand.) 5. Top with avocado and seeds of choice, and enjoy with 1-2 slices of whole wheat toast!

(B) Lunch
Option 1: Big Salad (mixed greens, raw broccoli finely-chopped, radishes, celery, red onion, cucumbers, tomatoes, AND 1 cup /130g canned/cooked beans or chickpeas), with 2-3 Tbs / 30-45 ml Olive Oil & Vinegar Dressing OR Linseed Oil & Dairy-Free Yogurt & Dijon Mustard Dressing
Whole grain crackers (2 oz / 57g) or a whole grain roll

Option 2: Beans and Greens soup*
Whole grain crackers (2 oz/57g) or 1 whole grain roll
Piece of fruit or 1 cup/230g cut fruit / berries
TIP: Make extra soup, and have it again for dinner.

Option 3: Chickpea Salad* Sandwich (see recipe with oil)
A pickle

Option 4: (**Midweek or Weekend Treat**): Shrimp Tacos (7-9 oz / 200-250g grilled or sautéed shrimp on 2 corn tortillas)
Chopped cabbage, ½ avocado, tomatoes, onions and peppers in tacos to taste
Black beans (1/2 cup/113g) or pinto beans (1/2 cup/113g)
Brown rice (1/2 cup/85g) (optional)

(B) Dinner
Option 1: Left-Over Beans & Greens Soup
Whole grain crackers (2 oz/57g) or 1 whole grain roll (optional)

Option 2: Whole Roasted Cauliflower & Tahini-Sauce Ingredients:
- 1 whole cauliflower
- 2 Tbs olive oil
- ½ teaspoon salt
- 1 Tbs mixed coriander and cumin
- 1 cup water
- 3-4 Tbs Tahini-sauce (1/2 cup or 4oz Tahini-paste; ¼-1/3 cup or 60-80ml warm water; 1-2 Tbs lemon juice; 1-2 Tbs olive oil but this is optional; 2 garlic cloves finely-minced; ½ teaspoon kosher salt; ¼ teaspoon pepper; if desired add a splash of soy sauce or liquid aminos)
- fresh herbs (for garnish) – parsley, dill, (and mint if desired)

Instructions: 1. Preheat oven to 425F/218C 2. Trim the cauliflower, either cutting off the stem or leaving it intact, but trimming the bottom enough so it stands up straight. 3. Place it in an ovenproof pan, skillet or "dutch oven." Pour 1Tbs of olive oil all over the

cauliflower, sprinkle with salt, coriander and cumin. Pour 1 cup of water into the bottom of the pan. 4. Cover tightly with foil or the lid, and bake for 45-60 minutes (or until tender all the way to the middle, when pierced with a knife). 5. Make the tahini (if you're not using store- bought), whisking together its ingrredients in a jar or bowl. 6. Carefully take the foil or lid off the baked cauliflower, drizzle with a bit more olive oil, and place uncovered back in the oven for ca. 30 minutes, rotating it halfway through. Roast until deeply golden. 7. Remove from the oven & sprinkle a bit more of the mixed spices if desired, the fresh herbs, and either drizzle the tahini-sauce over the whole thing, in the pan, or cut it up into wedges and serve the sauce on the side.
Enjoy with 1/3 a dinner plate of quinoa, buckwheat, or whole grain farro.

Option 3: (**Midweek or Weekend Treat**, if you haven't had it at lunch): Broiled Scallops OR Shrimp scampi* (4 oz/113g) with healthy pasta (1 cup/200g cooked)
Broccoli with lemon (at least 1 cup/91g)
Green salad (2 cups/50g greens with tomatoes and any other vegetables you like)
Vinaigrette-style dressing (2 Tbs/30ml)

Option 4: Spanokorizo* (Greek spinach and rice) (1-2 cups/115-230g)
White beans with garlic (1/2 cup/113g)
Green salad (2 cups/50g greens with tomatoes and any other vegetables you like) with Vinaigrette-style dressing (2 Tbs)

(B) Snack Options:
-Apple with peanut butter (1-2 Tbs/15-30g)
-Trail mix - raw nuts, seeds, and dried fruit (1/4 cup/43 g)
-Starbuck's Extra-Dry "Tall" (small) Cappucino with Oat, Soy, or Almond Milk
-Carrot- and celery-sticks with hummus, or homemade tofu dip (1/4 cup/43 g)
-(**Midweek & Weekend Treat Snacks**):
-**Air-popped popcorn** (see below) with seasoning of choice (3 cups/24g popped)
-**Berries & Mint Shake** (7 oz/200g frozen Mixed Berries; 1 cup / 250ml Oat-Milk unsweetened; 2-3 ice-cubes and/or water; fresh mint-leaves; add 1-2 dashes of liquid Stevia if desired)
-**Papaya & Watermelon Smoothie** (50g papaya, 100g watermelon, 1 Tbs lemon-juice, 2-3 ice cubes, blended)

Note about popcorn: air-popped uses only hot air to pop the kernels and is oil-free. Most microwave popcorn uses some oil for popping. If using, choose ones with the fewest additives, and ones that you know what all of the ingredients actually are. You can pop your own in the microwave without oil (just ad 1/3 cup kernels to a brown paper lunch bag, fold over the top and cook until the popping stops). Or pop in hot oil in the traditional way, if/when you are using oil.

Meal Plan (C)
Fast Day with Fish

*No meat, poultry, or dairy (both fish and shellfish is allowed), plus oil and wine is allowed. As far as Great Lent goes, this **(C)** fasting-rule applies to the feast of Annunciation when it happens during Lent (March 25 on the New Calendar or April 7 on the Older Calendar), and Palm Sunday. For **(C)**-days you can use the meals in **(A)** and **(B)** made with fish instead of the other protein-rich food like tofu or beans, plus:*

(C) Breakfast
Option 1: Oatmeal (1/2 cup / 57g uncooked)
Non-dairy milk of choice
Fresh or frozen fruit of choice (at least 1/2 cup/85-115g)
Nuts (1-2 oz/28-57 g)
If you are using dried fruit, try to select one without added sugar (1/4 cup/43g).

Option 2: Whole grain toast (1-2 slices)
Spread with hummus or nut butter of choice (1-2 Tbs/ 15-30ml.) OR
Slice of smoked salmon on top, garnished with fresh dill OR
Sliced or mashed avocado (1/2 average size fruit) or fruit spread of choice
Sesame, pumpkin or unshelled hemp seeds or furikake (a Japanese seasoning with sesame seeds and seaweed) sprinkled on top
Fruit (I piece or 1 cup/230g of cut fruit/berries)
Small container of non-dairy yogurt (optional)

(C) Lunch
Option 1: Tuna salad sandwich on whole grain bread (made with 1 average-size can tuna, 1- 2 Tbs egg-free mayonnaise)
Lettuce and tomato on the sandwich
Piece of fruit

Option 2: Grilled low-fat fish like cod, tilapia, flounder (6-7.5 oz / 170-213g)
Mashed Broccoli & Cauliflower (mash in blender or using a hand-mixer, with fresh dill and lemon juice, adding salt & pepper to taste, and garlic if desired)
Piece of fruit or small tossed-greens salad on the side

Option 3: Grilled Salmon Chunks (4 oz / 113g) on Large Green Salad (w 1-2 Tbs Viniagrette dressing)
Whole grain roll (1) or crackers (2 oz/57g) Piece of fruit

(C) Dinner
Option 1: Roasted salmon (4 oz / 113g) with Brussels sprouts (on ca. 1/4 of your plate)

Whole grain farro, brown rice, buckwheat or quinoa, (1/2 - 1 cup/85-170g or ca. ¼ of your plate) or a whole grain slice of bread

Option 2: Grilled low-fat fish like cod, tilapia, flounder (6-7.5 oz / 170-213g)
Roasted potatoes with lemon* (1 cup/140g) with green beans or broccoli or asparagus (roasted with potatoes) (1 cup/75g)

(C) Snack Options:
-Apple with peanut butter (1-2 Tbs/15-30g)
-Trail mix - raw nuts, seeds, and dried fruit (1/4 cup/43 g)
-Starbuck's Extra-Dry "Tall" (small) Cappucino with Oat, Soy, or Almond Milk
-Carrot- and celery-sticks with hummus, or homemade tofu dip (1/4 cup/43 g)
-**Air-popped popcorn** (see below) with seasoning of choice (3 cups/24g popped); OR
-**Berries & Mint Shake** (7 oz/200g frozen Mixed Berries; 1 cup / 250ml Oat-Milk unsweetened; 2-3 ice-cubes and/or water; fresh mint-leaves; add 1-2 dashes of liquid Stevia if desired)

Note about popcorn: air-popped uses only hot air to pop the kernels and is oil-free. Most microwave popcorn uses some oil for popping. If using, choose ones with the fewest additives, and ones that you know what all of the ingredients actually are. You can pop your own in the microwave without oil (just ad 1/3 cup kernels to a brown paper lunch bag, fold over the top and cook until the popping stops). Or pop in hot oil in the traditional way, if/when you are using oil.

Meal Plan (D)
Cheesefare/Maslenitsa Week

*No meat or poultry, but dairy-products, fish, caviar, shellfish, and oil and wine are allowed. This **(D)** fasting-rule applies to just one week in the church year: Cheesefare Week (or "Maslenitsa" in Russian), the entire week or the Monday-to-Sunday immediately preceding Lent. For **(D)**-type days you can use the meals in **(A), (B), and (C)** made with dairy-products instead of their non-dairy replacements (we suggest low-fat dairy for those watching their weight), and fish instead of the other protein-rich food like tofu or beans, plus:*

(D) Breakfast
Option 1: 1-2 slices whole grain toast with choice with butter (1 tsp/5g per slice)
Eggs, cooked to your liking (2)
Piece of cheese of choice (1-2 oz/28-56g) – if you are watching your weight, opt for 1oz/28g of a natural cheese like blue cheese, mozzarella, or feta
Fruit of choice (at least 1/2 cup/85-115g)

Option 2: Avocado & Egg on Rye Toast
2 slices of rye toast, each topped with: Bed of rocket-salad-leaves, 1/4 crushed avocado, and 1 poached egg. Salt & pepper to taste.

Option 3: Eggs (2) scrambled with spinach and mushrooms (or vegetables of choice)
Whole grain toast (1-2 slices) with butter (1 tsp/5g per slice)
Fresh fruit (at least 1 cup/230g cut fruit or berries, or 1 piece whole fruit)

Option 4: Melon & Cottage Cheese
½ melon, with 1 to 1 ½ portions (3-5 Tbs) cottage cheese
1-2 slices whole grain toast with choice of butter (1 tsp/5g per slice)

(D) Lunch
Option 1: Greek salad with beans and feta* OR
Big Salad (with mixed greens, celery, raw broccoli, red onion, radishes, etc.) and with 1 chopped boiled egg, 6-7 crushed walnut-halves and a low-fat dressing (2-3 Tbs 1% fat Yogurt & Dijon Mustard & some sugar-free soy sauce & fresh herbs)
Whole grain roll or whole grain pita bread (1)
Piece of fruit

Option 2: Bean and cheese burrito (1) or Tostada (2 corn tortillas) Toppings of salsa, tomatoes, avocado, onions, and hot sauce as desired
Piece of fruit or 1 cup cut fruit

Option 3: (**Midweek/Weekend Treat**) Blini/Blintzes with Toppings
1-2 "Blini" (try making them with whole wheat flour, if possible) each topped with 1 Tbs sour cream, and/or 1 teaspoon caviar, 1 Tbs chopped boiled egg, 1 piece herring or slice of smoked salmon, some chopped spring-onion

(D) Dinner

Option 1: Stuffed Eggplant (for 2 servings) Ingredients:
- 2 small eggplants
- 1 package (12oz/349g) Silk Tofu
- 1 egg-white, raw
- 1 onion
- 1 clove garlic
- 1 carrot, grated
- lemon juice
- vegetable bouillon-cube (or 1 Tbs)
- nutmeg
- finely chopped fresh herbs (parsley, dill, chives, etc.)

Instructions: 1. Preheat the oven to 338F or 170C. Wash the eggplants and slice each in half. 2. Spoon out the inside of the eggplant-halves so that an approximately ½-cm-wide frame remains. 3. Cut the spooned-out insides of the eggplant in cubes, and sprinkle with lemon. 4. Crush up the tofu in a bowl with a fork. Add crushed bouillon-cube, some nutmeg, pepper, and fresh herbs. 5. Sautee the onion and garlic briefly in a non-stick pan, then add the eggplant-cubes, grated carrot, and tofu-mix into the pan, and sautee further for ca. 2 minutes. 6. Empty the sauteed tofu-and-vegetables into a bowl, mix in the egg-white, and stuff the eggplant-halves with the tofu-and-vegetable stuffing. 7. Bake in the preheated oven for ca. 25 minutes.
Enjoy with a side of whole grain pasta or brown rice (optional)

Option 2: (**Midweek/Weekend Treat, if you didn't have this for lunch**) Blini/Blintzes with Toppings - 1-2 "Blini" (try making them with whole wheat flour, if possible) each topped with 1 Tbs sour cream, and/or 1 teaspoon caviar, 1 Tbs chopped boiled egg, 1 piece herring or slice of smoked salmon, some chopped spring-onion

Option 3: Zucchini-Noodles (Zoodles) with Cheese & Tomatoes,
On Bed of Arugula/Rocket-Salad
Instructions: Heat 1 Tbs of olive oil in a large saute pan or skillet over medium heat. Once the oil is hot, add one teaspoon garlic and 1 can strained (or 2 fresh, chopped tomatoes) and saute a minute or so. Add zucchini noodles and saute for 5 minutes, until just tender and al dente. Add ca. 1 handful crushed feta; Taste the noodles and season with salt and pepper as needed. Serve over a bed of arugula-salad, laid out on a plate. (NOTE: This dish can be made during Lent, using firm tofu instead of the cheese.)
1 whole grain roll or slice of whole grain bread (optional)

Option 4: Vegetarian Chili* (1.5 cups/300g)
Toppings: pickled onions, sour cream, cheese, tomatoes, ½ avocado
Green salad (2 cups/50g greens plus vegetables of choice and dressing)

(D) Snacks
Yogurt (small container) with fruit
Mozzarella (1oz /28g) & Tomato Caprese
Fruit and nuts/nut butter (1-2 oz/28-57g)
Vegetable-sticks with (low-fat) yogurt-dip (1-2oz/28-57g)
Midweek/Weekend Treat Snacks:
Popcorn with parmesan and Italian seasoning (3 cups/24g popped)
Creamed Berries (mix in a blender 7oz/200g mixed berries, 1-2 tblsp yogurt, some liquid- Stevia, and some lemon juice)

Meal Plan (E)
No Fasting Day

On (E)-type days, everything is allowed! Nonetheless, to HealthyFasters we suggest both easing into the Lenten fasting-season by adopting a healthy non-fasting diet (as suggested in the meal plan below) already in the pre-Lenten weeks, and maintaining it after Lent, so as not to lose the habit and benefits of the HealthyFast discipline. If you are watching your weight, opt for low-fat dairy-products, lean meats, and low-fat fish, all portioned. And have at least the minimal amount of vegetables at lunch and dinner, as well as at least two portions of fruit daily.

*NOTE: Before and after Lent, **more daily exercise** is recommended. That is to say, instead of the Lenten 20-30 minute daily brisk walk, treat yourself to a 40 min – 1 hour daily walk outside the fasting season!*

*Options for **(E)**-type meals include all-of-the-above **(A), (B), (C),** and **(D)**-options (so feel free to have oatmeal for breakfast on fast-free days!), plus:*

(E) Breakfast

Option 1: whole grain pancakes (2-3) with fruit compote
Turkey bacon, 2 slices
1 egg, cooked to taste (optional)
1 cup fruit (optional)

Option 2: Light Veggie-Omelette
Ingredients: 1 whole egg, 2-3 egg whites, ca. 3 1/2oz / 100g mushrooms & tomatoes or other vegetables, 1 chopped spring onion, vegetable broth, fresh herbs to garnish
Instructions: 1. whisk the eggs, spring onion, and salt & pepper in a bowl; 2. Cut up the vegetables and lightly sautee in a non-stick pan, using vegetable broth to avoid sticking; 3. Add the eggs and turn down the heat, and let cook for 1-2 minutes; 4. Flip over carefully with a large spatula, and cook for another 2 minutes; 5. Fold the omelette in half and serve with some chives and/or half a cherry-tomato on top!

Option 3: Yogurt (1 cup/245g) with at least 1 cup/230g fruit
Topped with granola (2 Tbs/28g)

Option 4: 2 slices whole wheat toast with 1 to 1 1/2 portion (3-5 Tbs) homemade cottage-cheese or "Quark/Topfen" spread (mixed with finely-chopped bell-pepper, seasoned with salt & herbs, or turmeric/curcuma & black pepper to taste; use low-fat cottage-cheese or "Quark" or "Topfen" – sold in German-speaking countries – if watching your weight)
1 cup berries or 1 piece fruit

(E) Lunch

Option 1: Salad with chicken breast, or turkey, or lean steak-pieces (3-4 oz/85-113g grilled or baked)
At least 2 cups/50g salad greens with 1 cup/130g vegetables of choice
Vinaigrette-style dressing or Light Yogurt-and-Dijon Mustard Dressing (2-3 Tbs/30-45ml) Whole grain roll, pita bread, or crackers (optional)

Option 2: Beef Teriyaki with Cauliflower-Rice (recipe for 2 portions) Ingredients:
- 12-14oz / 350-400g lean beef-strips
- 7oz / 200g cauliflower-rice, frozen
- 1 spring onion (green onion)
- 2 red bell peppers
- 2 carrots
- 1 tblsp chives, 1 tblsp coriander
- For the Teriyaki sauce: 1 small piece fresh ginger, grated; 1 clove garlic, minced; 1 small chili-pepper, cleaned and with seeds removed; ½ tblsp cumin; ½ tblsp lime- juice; several splashes sugar-free soy sauce; 1-2 dashes liquid Stevia
- Vegetable bouillon/broth (sugar and oil-free), salt & pepper

Instructions: 1. Cut the beef, bell-peppers, and green onion into thin strips; 2. Mix all the ingredients of the Teriyaki sauce well, in a large bowl. Immerse the beef-bell-peppers-and-green onion into this sauce, and marinate for 15-20 minutes; 3. In the meantime, place the cauliflower-rice in a preheated nonstick pan, letting it fry a bit. Then add vegetable bouillon/broth, turn the heat down and simmer for ca. 8 minutes; 4. Preheat another pan on high heat, pour in the now-marinated beef-with-sauce, letting it first fry a bit, then add some water and cook further over medium-heat for 8-10 minutes; 5. Serve the beef and cauliflower-rice side-by-side in broad, shallow bowls, seasoned with a bit of salt & pepper to taste, and garnished with fresh herbs.
1 piece fruit or 1 handful mixed berries (optional, unless you haven't had any fruit yet today!)

Option 3: Chicken and rice soup with avgolemono or spicy garlic oil (2 cups/500g)*
Whole grain roll, pita bread or crackers (optional)
Green salad (optional)

(E) Dinner

Option 1: Chicken and vegetable stir-fry (1-2 cups/210-420g) Brown rice or healthy whole grain (1/2 - 1 cup/85-170g) Edamame (1/2 cup/85g) (optional)

Option 2: Roast Chicken* (4 oz/115g) Roast sweet potatoes (1/2 - 1 cup/70-140g)
Cooked greens* or Greek green beans*

Option 3: Easy Stuffed Peppers (for 2 people or 2 portions)
Ingredients: 4 bell-peppers, lean ground-beef (12-14oz /350-400g), 2-3 finely-chopped onions,

minced garlic, salt&pepper, 1 tblsp Dijon-mustard, 1 eggwhite, dry or fresh marjoram.
Instructions: 1. Slice the tops off the peppers and clean the peppers, removing the seeds from inside; 2. Mix together the rest of the ingredients in a bowl, stuff the peppers with the mixture, and put the pepper-caps back on; 3. Wrap each pepper separately in aluminum foil, and bake in preheated oven at 200C or 392F for ca. 30 minutes; 4. Make a sauce of drained tomatoes, vegetable broth and/or sugar-free soy sauce, with additional herbs and salt & pepper as desired, letting it simmer in a pan while the peppers bake. Serve the peppers in a shallow pool of the sauce.
Small bowl of a whole wheat grain on the side (optional)

(E) Snacks
Yogurt (small container) with fruit
Mozzarella (1oz /28g) & Tomato Caprese
Fruit and nuts (a handful) or nut butter (ca 1oz/28g)
Starbucks Skinny "Tall" (small) Cappucino
Vegetable-sticks with (low-fat) yogurt-dip (1-2oz/28-57g)
Midweek/Weekend Treat Snacks:
Popcorn with parmesan and Italian seasoning (3 cups/24g popped)
Creamed Berries (blend 7oz/200g mixed berries, 1-2 tblsp yogurt, some liquid-Stevia, and some lemon juice)

Meal Plan (F)
Pascha! Transitioning from Fasting to Feasting

While the joyous Paschal night is no time to be obsessing over calories, we do want to go slow with regard to the rich foods, as our bodies are not used to them. The following options are suggested for Pascha-night and the ensuing Bright Week, – not to make any HealthyFasters feel guilty about having traditional Paschal foods, like glazed ham or sausages/kolbasa or cheese-Pascha (syrnaya pascha in the Russian tradition) or Pascha-cookies or something else, – but just to offer some helpful tips and little "tricks" (like including a healthy dose of vegetables to balance our meals, replacing mashed potatoes with mashed cauliflower, keeping the meats lean when we can, and taking it easy with alcohol, choosing dry white wine over heavier drinks if we drink alcohol). AND REMEMBER: After we rest from the rigorous services of Great/Holy/Strastnaya Week and celebrate Pascha-Sunday and Monday, more daily exercise is recommended. That is to say, instead of the Lenten 20-30 minute daily brisk walk, treat yourself to a 40 min-1 hour daily walk in the springtime sun (or rain)!

(F) Late Night/Early Morning - after Divine Liturgy
Hard boiled egg - of course!
Avoglemono soup* or chicken and rice soup*
Whole grain roll/cracker with 1oz piece of your favorite cheese, OR Pascha bread OR Pascha cookie OR 1-2 tblsp cheese-Pascha (optional)
Glass of dry white wine (optional) – if you have two glasses, drink one large glass of water in between

(F) Light Brunch on Pascha-Sunday
Iced Coffee (Low-fat milk, instant coffee-powder, 3 ice-cubes, liquid Stevia, mixed in a blender and sprinkled with cinnamon or coffee-powder) OR just coffee
Handful of berries with 1-2 tblsp cheese-Pascha OR atop low-fat yogurt

(F) Late Lunch - feast meal
Lamb, ham, turkey or festival meat of choice (3-4 oz/85-115g)
Roast or mashed potatoes (1/2 - 1 cup/70-140g) OR mashed cauliflower with 1-2 tblsp low- fat yogurt mixed in OR grilled asparagus
Salad (at least 1-2 cups/20g - 140g) with Viniagrette or Low-fat Yogurt-Dressing Dessert of choice (a small portion to avoid stomach upset)
Glass of dry white wine (optional) – if you have two glasses, drink one large glass of water in between

(F) Dinner - probably another feast meal
Reasonable portion of meat (3-4 oz/85-115g) - keep it lean to avoid stomach upset
Cooked Vegetables (at least 1-2 cups/20g-14og. Try grilled brussels sprouts, glazed with olive oil and salt!)
Small Salad
Reasonable portion of dessert
Glass of dry white wine (optional) – if you have two glasses, drink one large glass of water in between

(F) Breakfast, Lunch and Dinner During Bright Week – see Meal-Plan **(E)**

Recipes
for
Lent, and Any Other Season!

Denise Canellos, MS, CNS

*HEALTHY*FAST* RECIPES
Denise Canellos, MS, CNS

NOTE: More Lenten recipes are included within the Meal Plans above.

About the recipes below, some notes from Denise:

- *These recipes may look long, but they do not take much time. Each small step is listed, so even the most inexperienced cook can prepare these dishes well.*
- *The salt amounts reflect Morton Kosher Salt for cooking and table salt for baking; If you use regular table salt, cut the amounts in half. If you use a coarser salt such as Diamond Crystal Kosher salt, use 1.5 times the salt listed.*
- *Please take these recipes and make them your own. They are all starting points and techniques for delicious, healthy cooking. Most of them have a Mediterranean flavor profile because that is how I usually cook. If you like different spices and herbs, use your favorites.*

I wholeheartedly believe we can dramatically reduce chronic disease and chronic pain by eating this way. We can start a nutrition revolution, bringing us back to the natural, healthy foods we were designed to eat.

- Main Courses & Salads -

Steel Cut Oats: Cook Once and Eat All Week
For 8 servings; 10 minutes
Ingredients:
- 2 cups/226 g steel-cut oats
- 8 cups/2 liters of water
- 2 pinches of salt

Instructions:
1. Place all ingredients in a pot with a lid, and bring to a boil, uncovered.
2. Give it a few good stirs, turn off the heat, and cover the pot.
3. Let sit overnight on the stove or counter.
4. In the morning, give it a good stir. Place as much as you want for breakfast in a bowl to heat, and save the remainder in the refrigerator for the rest of the week.
5. Add 1 Tbs flax meal (ground flax) and fruit, and reheat in the microwave. You don't have to worry about it boiling over since it's already cooked. You can add chopped apples and cinnamon for a terrific bowl of apple-pie oats.

Pumpkin seeds or sliced almonds are also great toppings; they are crunchy and give us a little boost of healthy fat and protein. Cinnamon and vanilla are more great options, as spices give us a boost of anti-inflammatory compounds too.

Big Salad

This is my go-to lunch salad. I don't measure anything, and just eyeball how much I need, depending on how many people I'm feeding. You will quickly get the hang of making salads this way. Serves 2 generously; 10-20 minutes (depending on whether you buy pre-chopped vegetables!)

Ingredients:
- Cauliflower finely chopped, or purchase cauliflower "rice"
- Steamed lentils, or canned beans that you've rinsed (or 1 chopped boiled egg on not- fasting days)
- Chopped scallions (2-3), or anything oniony
- Cherry or grape tomatoes, or a chopped big tomato
- Any other vegetables you like, such as celery, broccoli, or peppers
- Avocado, chopped
- Lemon juice (1 lemon)
- Extra Virgin Olive Oil (optional, can use oil-free dressing with Non Dairy or Lowfat Dairy Yogurt on fast-free days)
- Salt and pepper

Instructions:
1. Take out a big bowl, and add about half of the bag of cauliflower.
2. Add half the package of lentils or can of beans.
3. Add the scallions, tomatoes, and any other vegetables you want.
4. Squeeze a little lemon juice over the chopped avocado and the rest over the salad.
5. Add an equal amount of olive oil/or oil-free dressing to the salad and toss.
6. (Taste and adjust the lemon juice and oil/oil-free dressing until it tastes great.)
7. Sprinkle on some salt and pepper.
8. Place the avocado on top when you're ready to serve.

Note: If I've made some farro, quinoa or brown rice I'll throw that in, or substitute it for either the lentils or the cauliflower.

Easy Bean and Tuna Salad, Mediterranean Style

Serves 2 people generously (easily doubles); 10 minutes

Ingredients:
- 1 can (14.5 oz/411 g) white kidney beans or chickpeas, drained and rinsed
- 2 cans (5 oz/142 g) tuna packed in olive oil, drained
- 1 small or 1/2 large avocado, diced
- 1 cup/200 g cherry tomatoes, halved
- 1/2 red onion, chopped or 3-4 scallions, sliced thin
- 2-3 radishes, sliced thin (Add the tops, too, if you have them)
- Juice of 1/2–1 lemon
- Extra virgin olive oil, about twice as much as lemon juice
- 1-2 Tbs/2-3 g chopped parsley
- Salt and pepper

Instructions:
1. Squeeze lemon onto the avocado to prevent browning.
2. Combine all the ingredients and toss.
3. Add salt and pepper to taste.

You can easily double this salad. Add any other veggies you like and leave out what you don't. It keeps for 2-3 days in the fridge and travels well.

Scoop some salad onto lettuce leaves or baby spinach for a hearty salad, or stuff into a whole-wheat pita pocket for a quick, delicious sandwich. It's also good on top of some whole wheat crackers or as a topping in a brown rice bowl.

Variation: Easy Taco Salad
- Substitute black beans for the white beans and substitute corn for the tuna.
- Use sliced red onion.
- Add chopped bell pepper.
- Substitute lime juice instead of lemon juice in the dressing.
- Top with cilantro instead of parsley.
- Salad greens for serving
- Tortilla chips and salsa (optional)
- Combine all ingredients as in the Easy Bean and Tuna Salad and enjoy.

Variation #2: Even Easier

Toss black beans with store-bought pico de gallo, chopped avocado and canned corn and make veggie tacos, burritos or a taco salad.

Barley and Wilted Spinach Salad

Serves 2 as a main dish, 4 as a side; 20 minutes Ingredients:
- 2 Tbs/28 g extra virgin olive oil
- 1 cup/113 g quick-cooking barley
- 1 small onion, finely chopped
- 2 cloves garlic, minced
- pinch of red pepper flakes
- 1 medium size lemon
- 1 3/4 cups/ 236 g water
- 2 6oz./9 g bags spinach, roughly chopped
- parmesan cheese, grated or shaved, to garnish the top (on fast-free days); OR handful of crushed, raw walnuts

Instructions:
1. In a large saucepan, heat olive oil over medium-high heat until hot.
2. Zest your lemon, then cut it in half around the middle.
3. Cook the lemon halves, cut side down, in the hot oil until brown, about 1-2 minutes.
4. Set lemons aside for later.
5. Add your onion, garlic, red pepper flakes, and barley to the oil and cook, stirring often, until barley is lightly toasted and onion is soft.
6. Add water and 1/2 tsp of salt, bring to a boil; then turn the heat down, cover and simmer for 10 minutes. Barley will be almost done.
7. Add your spinach and 1 tsp of the lemon zest, stir and continue to cook until spinach wilts and the barley is tender.
8. Add salt and pepper to taste.
9. Top with Parmesan cheese (either grated or shavings) OR crushed raw walnuts.
10. Done! Serve hot, warm, or at room temperature.

You can also add a can of drained, rinsed beans like garbanzo or cannellini beans for a more substantial salad.

This salad keeps for a few days in the refrigerator and makes a great lunch the next day.

Avgolemono Soup (Greek lemon and egg soup)
This soup is nourishing and comforting, easy on a sore throat and a tender tummy.
Serves 4; 30 minutes total, 15 active
Ingredients:
- 1 Tbs/14 g extra virgin olive oil
- 1 small onion, diced
- 1 carrot, diced
- 1 celery rib, diced
- 4 cups/1 liter (1 quart) chicken broth
- 1/2 cup/ 56 g long grain white rice
- 2 eggs
- Juice of one large or two small lemons
- Salt and pepper

Instructions:
1. Start by heating the olive oil in your soup pot.
2. Add the vegetables and cook until they are very soft.
3. Add all 4 cups chicken broth and bring to a gentle boil.
4. Add ½ cup of rice (white tastes best here) and simmer until the rice is tender about 15 minutes.
5. While the soup simmers, beat two eggs in a medium-sized bowl and add the juice of one large or two small lemons.
6. Whisk again until completely blended.
7. When the rice is tender, turn off the heat on the soup and add a ladle full of the hot soup to the eggs and lemon juice.
8. Whisk, and then add another ladle of hot soup to the egg mixture, stirring it. This should bring the eggs up to temperature, so they will not seize when they hit the soup.
9. Add the egg mixture to the soup pot, and stir until combined and the soup is creamy.
10. Season to taste and you are done!

Tempering the eggs sounds complicated, but it is really quite simple, and once you do it the first time it will be a breeze.

Lentil and Vegetable Soup (with or without oil)
This soup is warm, filling, and comforting. Do not skip the vinegar or lemon juice at the end – it brightens the flavor. Serves 6-8; 60 minutes, 15 active
Ingredients:
- 1 lb./453 g dried lentils (brown or green), no need to soak
- ¼ cup/60 ml olive oil (optional) OR oil-free vegetable broth
- 1 cup/ 150 g chopped onions
- 2 large stalks celery, chopped
- 1 large carrot, chopped

- 2 cloves garlic, minced or crushed
- 1 Tbs/ 14 g tomato paste (I use the kind in the tube.)
- ½ – 1 tsp/2 g dried oregano
- 1 bay leaf
- 2 quarts/liters water
- ¼ cup/4 g chopped fresh parsley
- 3 Tbs/ 45 ml red wine vinegar or lemon juice

Instructions:
1. Rinse lentils in cold water and drain them, they don't need to be soaked overnight.
2. Heat olive oil OR vegetable broth in a large saucepan or soup pot, over medium heat.
3. Add onions, celery, and carrot, and saute until soft. Add vegetable broth as needed to avoid sticking.
4. Add garlic and cook for another 30 seconds or so, until you can smell it.
5. Add tomato paste, oregano, and bay leaf, cook until tomato paste darkens a little.
6. Add lentils and stir to coat with the vegetables and tomato paste.
7. Add water and bring to a boil.
8. Lower heat to a simmer and cook, loosely covered, for 30 minutes, then add 1/2 tsp salt.
9. Simmer for another 15 minutes or so, until lentils are fully tender.
10. Stir in lemon juice or vinegar, add salt and pepper to taste.

This is the traditional dish served in Greek households on the first Monday of Great Lent, called Clean Monday. When the soup is this good, we can eat "clean" all of the time!

Magic Bean Soup (with oil)

This soup is so good, filling, and comforting it just feeds the soul. Some toasted ciabatta bread is great alongside. Serves 8; 2 hours, 20 minutes active

Ingredients:
- 1 lb/453 g dried cannellini beans
- 2 bay leaves
- 2 sprigs of thyme
- 2 Tbs/17 g salt
- 6 Tbs/ 89 ml olive oil
- Leftover rind from Parmesan cheese (optional, on not fasting days)
- 6 cloves garlic, sliced
- 1 tsp/1-2 g red pepper flakes
- Grated Parmesan cheese to serve (optional, on not fasting days)
- 8 oz./ 30 g Greens such as arugula or spinach

Instructions:
1. Fill a deep bowl with water, add 2 Tbs of salt, stir to dissolve.
2. Add beans to the bowl and soak overnight (or at least 8 hours).
3. Drain the beans, add to a big, heavy pot (a stockpot type) with about 4 quarts/liters of water.
4. Drop in two bay leaves, a few sprigs of thyme, and 1 Tbs olive oil.
5. Bring the beans to a boil and simmer for an hour with the lid just a little ajar; stir every now and then to keep the beans from sticking to the bottom. (The soup won't look very good yet, but don't despair.)

6. Now add 2 teaspoons of salt, some pepper, (and a piece or two of parmesan cheese rind if using).
7. Continue to simmer with the lid off, until the beans are tender and the soup is the texture you like.
8. Heat a small skillet on medium-high, add 4 Tbs olive oil.
9. Add garlic and red pepper flakes (this amount will not make the soup spicy, just tasty – adjust to your taste).
10. When the garlic is sizzling and fragrant, add a ladle or two full of the soup broth and let it all bubble together in the skillet for a minute.
11. Add the olive oil mixture to the soup. The starch from the beans will help emulsify the flavored oil throughout the soup.
12. Let it all simmer for five minutes.
13. Remove the bay leaves and thyme stems.
14. Ladle half of the soup into a bowl to cool and then put it in the freezer to save for another day.
15. Add greens to hot soup and let them wilt.
16. Drizzle each bowl of soup with olive oil and sprinkle with parmesan cheese (if using) before serving.

Other add-ins could be leftover roasted vegetables such as red peppers, onions, eggplant – just add them and simmer together for a few minutes to warm the vegetables through. You also could add some delicious spring vegetables such as asparagus, peas, and baby carrots. Cook them with the olive oil and garlic mixture, then add to the soup and simmer until tender.

Your imagination is the only limit to this fabulous soup. You could even add tomatoes, zucchini, shrimp, or anything you think might be delicious.

Cooking Tender Greens (with oil)

Tender greens include spinach, Swiss chard, beet greens, and escarole. Serves 2 people generously; 10 minutes

Ingredients:
- 1 generous Tbs./15 ml olive oil
- 1 clove of garlic, smashed and peeled
- 1 pound/60 g tender greens, any tough stems removed; dice the stems from Swiss chard and saute them in the oil before adding the greens.)
- Juice from ½ a lemon
- Salt and pepper

Instructions:
1. Heat oil in a large, deep skillet over medium heat.
2. Add garlic, and saute until just golden.
3. Remove garlic clove with a slotted spoon or tongs, discard.
4. Add greens to skillet, toss with tongs to coat with the oil.
5. Cook greens until wilted.
6. Remove from the heat and add lemon juice.
7. Salt and pepper to taste.

Optional additions:
- About ¼ tsp/1-2 g red pepper flakes added to the oil with the garlic.
- A chopped shallot or small onion, added after you remove the garlic.
- Chopped tomatoes.
- A can of drained and rinsed beans.

Cooking Hearty Greens (with or without oil)
Hearty greens include collard, kale, and turnip greens.
Serves 2 generously; 45 minutes, 10 active
Ingredients:
- 1 generous Tbs./15 ml olive oil (optional)
- 2 cloves garlic, smashed
- 1/2 tsp/ 1 g red pepper flakes
- 2 bunches hearty greens
- 1 tsp/ 6 g salt

Instructions:
1. Place all ingredients into a large pot.
2. Add enough water to cover the greens by about 1 inch.
3. Bring to a boil over high heat.
4. Reduce heat and simmer, partially covered, for about 30 minutes.
5. Stir occasionally to prevent greens from sticking to the bottom of the pot.
6. Uncover and continue to simmer until greens are tender.
7. Drain the greens to serve, but save the liquid to use in place of vegetable stock.
8. Salt and pepper to taste.

Ratatouille (with oil) Two Ways:
in the Slow Cooker or Oven
This is also great over polenta and leftovers are a great topping for a baked potato. Mix in a can or two of cannellini beans or chickpeas if you want to make it more substantial.
Serves 4; 20 active minutes
Ingredients:
- 2 large onions, chopped
- 2-3 eggplants, peeled and chopped into 1"/2.5 cm pieces
- 3 zucchini, chopped into 1"/2.5 cm pieces
- 3 red, yellow, orange, or green bell peppers, chopped into 1"/2.5 cm pieces
- 4-5 tomatoes, chopped roughly
- 4 cloves of garlic, chopped or pressed
- 2 Tbs./28 g tomato paste
- 1 Tbs/14 g anchovy paste, or 3 anchovies, minced (optional)
- 4 Tbs./60 ml olive oil
- Red pepper flakes to taste
- 1 tsp/2 g dried oregano
- 1 tsp/2 g dried or 1Tbs/2.7 g fresh thyme
- 1 Tbs/ 2.7g fresh basil, sliced thinly
- Salt and pepper

Instructions for Slow Cooker:
1. You will want to skip this step but don't. It only takes a few minutes and really elevates the dish. Heat 2 Tbs olive oil in a skillet, and add the onions and a pinch of salt.
2. Cook until the onions are golden brown and soft, then add the tomato paste (and anchovy paste or anchovies), a good pinch of red pepper flakes, the oregano, and thyme.
3. Cook for a few minutes so the flavors meld.
4. While the onion mixture is cooking, chop the other vegetables and put them into the slow cooker. Add the remaining 2 Tbs of olive oil and 1 tsp of salt to the slow cooker.
5. Add onion mixture to slow cooker and stir to coat the vegetables with the onions.
6. Cook on high for 4 hours or on low for 5-6 hours.
7. If it is too soupy when finished, cook an additional 30 minutes with the lid off.
8. Top with the sliced basil and a drizzle of olive oil. Red wine or balsamic vinegar adds a nice touch too.

Oven Method:
1. Heat oven to 400° F/200° C.
2. Cook onions, salt, tomato paste (and anchovies) in oil (see steps 1-3 in the slow cooker version), just in a Dutch oven instead of a skillet.
3. Add eggplant and tomatoes to Dutch oven; top with a healthy pinch of salt.
4. Cook uncovered for 45 minutes, then remove from oven and give it all a good stir; add the zucchini and peppers.
5. Put the pot back into the oven and cook another 20-25 minutes, until a paring knife can cut through the vegetables easily.
6. Season with salt and pepper to taste.
7. Top with basil and a drizzle of olive oil. A splash of red wine vinegar adds a nice brightness, too.

Farro "Risotto" with Tomatoes
Serves 4; 35 minutes, 15 active
Ingredients:
- 2 cups/380 g farro
- 4 cups/ 1 liter water
- 1 medium onion, quartered and sliced
- 2 pints/560 g cherry tomatoes, halved, or chopped tomatoes
- 4 cloves garlic, sliced
- 1/4 tsp/1 g red pepper flakes (or more if you like it spicy)
- 2 Tbs/28 g olive oil
- 1 can (14.5 oz./411 g) cannellini beans, drained and rinsed
- 1 6oz./60 g package baby spinach
- 1 tsp/6 g kosher salt or 1/2 tsp/3 g table salt
- 2 TBS chopped fresh basil, optional
- Grated parmesan cheese for serving (optional)

Instructions:
1. Put the farro and the water into a stockpot or large saucepan, let soak while you prep the rest of the ingredients.
2. Slice the onion and add to the pot.
3. Halve or chop the tomatoes and add them to the pot.
4. Slice the garlic cloves and add them to the pot.
5. Add olive oil, red pepper flakes and salt to the pot.
6. Bring the pot to a boil.
7. Reduce heat and simmer for 30 minutes.
8. Stir the pot every 5-10 minutes to make sure nothing is sticking to the pot.
9. Add the beans to the pot.
10. Simmer vigorously until most of the liquid has evaporated, about 5 minutes.
11. Add spinach to the pot and stir to wilt.
12. Add basil, if using (it is worth it!)
13. Top each serving with grated cheese if desired, and a drizzle of olive oil.

Stir Fry with Peanut Sauce and Crispy Tofu (with oil & fish sauce)

This is my favorite stir-fry because this sauce is substantial, spicy and savory without being too salty. Just about any vegetable will work well here — so will rice or noodles. The cooking technique will vary depending on which grain you choose. This looks like it will take a long time to prepare, but it actually doesn't. Once you've cooked it once or twice it becomes a super quick meal. Serves 4; 30 minutes

Ingredients:

Sauce

- 2 tsp/9 g toasted sesame oil
- 4 Tbs/ 120 ml low-sodium soy sauce or tamari
- 1 Tbs/14 g Korean gochujang or Sriracha sauce (hot sauce)
- 1 tsp/ 5 ml fish sauce
- 1/2 cup/ 120 g peanut butter, can substitute almond butter
- 2-4 Tbs/30 - 60g water

Stir-Fry

- 1 14-15 oz/400-425 g package firm tofu, sliced into bite-sized planks and drained on paper towels.
- 4 cups/300 g chopped vegetables to stir fry: green beans, asparagus, broccoli, or kale.
- Rice, soba or udon noodles, to serve.
- 2 Tbs/28 g neutral cooking oil, such as grapeseed or canola

Instructions:

If you are serving over rice:

1. Mix the sesame oil, soy sauce or tamari, fish sauce, and water in a bowl.
2. Add the gochujang and whisk until blended.
3. Add the peanut butter and warm in the microwave for 30 seconds to 1 minute to melt.
4. Whisk the sauce and set aside.
5. Cook rice according to package directions and set aside.
6. Heat 1 Tbs cooking oil over high heat in a skillet or wok.

7. Add tofu to the skillet and let it sit until browned and crisp on the bottom. Do not flip too early or the tofu will stick to the pan.
8. Flip tofu over and cook on the other side.
9. Remove tofu from pan onto a plate and set aside.
10. Add 1 Tbs cooking oil to the skillet.
11. Add the vegetables and stir fry until crisp-tender, stirring most of the time.
12. If vegetables are not cooking quickly enough, add 2 Tbs water to the pan and cover it for 5 minutes.
13. Add the sauce to the skillet, stir to combine and warm through.
14. Add tofu back to the skillet and stir to coat with the sauce.
15. Serve with rice.

If you are using udon or soba noodles:
1. Put a large saucepan of water on to boil.
2. Heat 1 Tbs cooking oil over high heat in a skillet or wok.
3. Cook tofu as in the previous recipe.
4. Mix the sesame oil, soy sauce or tamari, and fish sauce together.
5. Add the gochujang and whisk until blended.
6. Add to your skillet or wok, place over low heat.
7. Add the peanut butter and warm through to melt the peanut butter.
8. Whisk the sauce and turn off the heat.
9. Add the vegetables to boiling water and cook to crisp-tender.
10. When done, fish out with a spider or tongs and add to skillet.
11. Bring the water back to a boil and cook noodles according to package directions.
12. Add cooked noodles to skillet. The water clinging to the noodles will help thin the sauce.
13. Turn on the heat under the skillet to medium-high to warm everything through.
14. Add tofu back to the skillet and stir to coat with sauce.

You can top with chopped peanuts, chopped scallions, and/or red pepper flakes.

Meal Sized Salad

This is a technique rather than a recipe. Grab whatever you have in each category and make a salad that's a meal. Hearty salads like these pack, travel and keep well. Lunch just got easy.

Serves 4-6; 15 minutes

1. Grab some baby spinach or mixed greens.
2. Microwave frozen cooked quinoa, rice (the brown, red and wild combo is really good), or grab some cooked farro, wheat berries or barley. Or use quick-cook grains.
3. Open a can of beans, rinse and drain, or open a package of cooked edamame from the deli, or defrost frozen edamame.
4. Toss in any nuts you want, unsalted nuts are best in a salad. If you use the candied ones, don't tell me about it.
5. Add whatever veggies you have around. Roasted peppers and artichoke hearts come ready to go in jars. Cucumber, cherry tomatoes, zucchini, onions, and

broccoli can be bought already cut or only take a minute to chop. Use whatever you like and have on hand.
6. Slice an avocado, add your cheese if not fasting, and toss with dressing.
- Honestly, preparing this should take you about 15 minutes, if you make your own dressing. You can make a lot for a crowd, or keep your ingredients separate and ready in the fridge for days' worth of great salads. Rinsed beans and cooked grains last for several days in the fridge, so do most vegetables. Cut the avocado right before serving, or toss slices with lemon juice so they don't brown.

Stuffed Peppers (with oil)
Serves 4 as a main dish; 60 minutes
Ingredients:
- 8 bell peppers, I like red or yellow, you can choose your color
- 2 cups/500 g cooked grains, like farro or rice
- 1 cup/ 225 g Marinara sauce (from a jar is fine)
- 1 can (14.5oz./411 g) lentils or white beans, drained and rinsed
- 2 Tbs/28 g olive oil
- Parmesan cheese, grated, about 1/2 cup (optional)

Instructions:
1. Cut tops off the peppers, scoop out the insides and trim a little off the bottom so they will stand up.
2. Preheat oven to 475° F/245° C.
3. Place peppers upside down in a pan so they fit snugly, and roast for 20 minutes.
4. Remove peppers from oven, turn right side up, and set aside.
5. Mix grains, sauce, beans or lentils, half of the grated cheese (if using) and olive oil.
6. Salt and pepper filling to taste. Add any other herbs or spices you like.
7. Stuff peppers with the filling.
8. Top with remaining grated cheese, if using.
9. Place filled peppers into a baking dish and bake for 15-20 minutes.

Peppers are done when they are hot all the way through, and the top is browned. This recipe also works for stuffed tomatoes. When I was growing up we usually had stuffed peppers and tomatoes together. Just scoop out the insides of the tomatoes, and add the pulp to your filling. Choose the big beefsteak tomatoes for stuffing, the heirloom tomatoes taste great but won't hold up in the oven.

Roasted Potatoes with Lemon (with oil or butter)
Serves 6 - adjusts easily for more or fewer servings; 60-75 minutes; 15 active
Ingredients:
- 6 medium to large Yukon Gold potatoes
- 2 Tbs butter (optional)
- 2 Tbs/28 g olive oil - double if not using butter
- 1 cup chicken stock OR vegetable stock
- 1 lemon, juiced
- 2 tsp/2 g dried oregano
- Salt and pepper

Instructions:
1. Heat oven to 425° F/220°C.
2. Peel the potatoes and slice 8 wedges lengthwise from each potato.
3. Place potatoes into a large bowl and add the stock, lemon juice, oregano, salt, pepper and 1 Tbs/14 g of the olive oil.
4. Put rest of the olive oil (and butter if using) in your roasting pan and place it in the hot oven to preheat.
5. Once the pan is hot, add the potato mixture to the pan. The pan will be hot, so use oven mitts.
6. Stir the potatoes every 15 minutes or so; they will be done in 45-60 minutes. You will know they are done when they are soft and getting brown in spots.
7. Taste to see if they need more salt or pepper. Enjoy!

Greek Style Vegetables (with oil)

This recipe serves about six people as a side, adjust as you need to and you don't have to be too fussy with the exact amounts — it all comes out fine in the end. You can cook the vegetables in the oven or on the stove. Serves 6 as a side; 30 minutes, 10 active

Ingredients:
- One large or two small onions, chopped
- 1 14.5 oz./411 g can diced tomatoes, or 1 8 oz./225 g can tomato sauce or 2 cups/400 g chopped fresh tomatoes.
- 1 pound green beans, trimmed or 1 pound summer squash, chopped into bite-size pieces (or both). You can use frozen green beans here, but I wouldn't use canned.
- 2 Tbs/30 ml olive oil, plus more to drizzle at the end
- 1 tsp/ 1 g dried oregano
- Lemon juice, optional
- Salt and pepper
- 1 handful fresh chopped parsley, optional

Instructions:
1. Heat oven to 325°F/165°C if cooking in the oven.
2. Warm 2 Tbs/28 g olive oil in a large skillet or saucepan over medium-high heat
3. Add onions and a good pinch of salt and cook until soft, about 5 minutes.
4. Add tomatoes, green beans, and/or squash.
5. Add oregano, a pinch of salt, and pepper – go easy on the salt, you can always add more.
6. Add enough water so tomato mixture almost covers the vegetables, about ½ cup.
7. Simmer, uncovered, either on the stove or in the oven for about 20 minutes.
8. Add fresh chopped parsley, and salt and pepper to taste. The juice of half a lemon is a good addition too — it really brightens the flavors.

If you want to make it more substantial, you can add some small potatoes. Add more tomatoes and a little more water and cook for an extra 20 minutes to make sure the potatoes are tender.

Roasted Vegetables w Oil (with or without Salmon)

This is more a technique than a set recipe. Almost any vegetable can be roasted to bring out its sweetness, and the crispy-crunchy texture wins over even staunch vegetable haters.
Serves 4-6, can be easily doubled; 25-65 minutes, depends on vegetables
Ingredients:
- Any fresh vegetable, from eggplant to zucchini, cut into bite-sized chunks. Asparagus can be left whole, so can mushrooms, cherry tomatoes, green beans, and anything else you would serve whole. (See our Whole Cauliflower-with-Tahini Sauce recipe in Meal Plan (A) above!) Potatoes and sweet potatoes can be cut into wedges or chopped into chunks.
- Olive oil to coat vegetables
- Salt and pepper
- Salmon filets, 3-4oz./85-100g) per person (optional)

Instructions:
1. Preheat your oven to 425° F/220° C.
2. Coat a baking sheet (or two, depending on how many vegetables you have) with non-stick spray or brush with oil.
3. Toss your vegetables with some olive oil, salt (kosher or coarse if you have it), and pepper. Vegetables need seasoning to bring out their flavors, so don't be afraid to add some salt.
4. Place vegetables on baking sheets in a single layer.
5. Put into the oven and roast until brown and they smell good. (Asparagus takes about 15 minutes, sweet potatoes about 45 minutes, other veggies fall somewhere in between.)
6. If adding salmon, add it to pan skin side down, 10 minutes before the vegetables will be done. They will be starting to brown at this point.
7. When vegetables are done, add optional seasonings (see below).

Suggested seasonings:
- Balsamic and red wine vinegar are great on summer vegetables like eggplant, bell peppers, and zucchini.
- Green veggies like broccoli love lemon juice; the acid balances the sweetness that comes out through roasting.
- Garlic is great, too—chop and mix into veggies on the hot pan so it cooks a little.
- Any herb you like works here, too. Red pepper flakes are great if you like a little heat.

I like to make a big batch of these and use them throughout the week. Then:
- Add to cooked pasta, quinoa, farro, or brown rice and top with vinegarette dressing for a great salad. Can also be combined with beans and cheese — double yum.
- Saute onions, garlic, (and a little anchovy paste if desired), add tomatoes and make a thick, chunky tomato sauce. Add roasted veggies and a little balsamic vinegar for a delicious stew.
- Add roasted vegetables to marinara sauce; top pasta or polenta with a filling, healthy and delicious sauce.
- Pack into a whole-wheat pita pocket with some hummus and greens for a great sandwich.

- Warm with some vegetable stock, and blend with leftover roasted vegetables for a comforting, creamy soup.
- Top greens with veggies and beans for a tasty, not boring salad.

Vegetarian Chili (with oil)

Serves 4; 45 minutes

Ingredients:
- 1 onion, chopped
- 1 Tbs/15 ml olive or grape seed oil
- 2 cloves garlic, chopped
- 1 Tbs/ 6 g ground cumin
- 2 tsp/ 2 g dried oregano
- 2 Tbs/ 12 g chili powder
- 1/4 tsp/ 0.25 g cayenne pepper – or to taste
- 1 lb/ 450 g vegetarian ground "meat" (optional)
- 1 14-15 oz/411 g can tomato sauce, no salt added if you can find it
- 1 teaspoon salt, or to taste
- 1/4 cup/28 g masa or corn flour, or fine ground cornmeal
- 2 15oz/411 g cans of beans (kidney, pinto or black beans), drained and rinsed
- 1 15 oz/411 g can diced tomatoes with green chilis, like Ro-Tel
- Optional: pickled onions (see next recipe)

Instructions:
1. Heat oil in a Dutch oven or stockpot over medium heat, and saute onion until translucent.
2. Add garlic, spices, and veggie crumbles, and saute until blended and veggie crumbles are hot.
3. Add beans and tomato sauce, swish out can with 1/4 cup water, pour it in, and bring to a low boil.
4. Cover the pot and simmer about 20 minutes to meld the flavors.
5. Make the pickled onions (see next recipe) if using, and set aside.
6. Mix the masa with 1/2 cup of water, and add to chili; let simmer uncovered a few minutes.
7. Add tomatoes with chilis, heat through.

Enjoy chili with your favorite toppings, like pickled onions, chopped red onions, avocado, (or grated cheese on not-fasting days).

Easy Pickled Onions - Best Chili Topping
- 1 red onion, halved and sliced into fairly thin strips
- Juice of 1-2 limes (depending on their size and juiciness)
- 2 Pinches of salt
- Pinch of sugar
1. Mix all ingredients in a small bowl and let sit while you make the chili.
2. Add enough lime juice to come about halfway up the onions, stir.
3. The onions need about 20 minutes to get pickled.

Leftover pickled onions will last for about a week in the fridge and are fantastic on a sandwich or salad.

Spanakorizo (Spinach and Rice with oil)
Serves 4-6, 30 minutes
Ingredients:
- 2 medium onions, chopped finely
- 1/2 cup/118 ml olive oil
- 1 Tbs/14 g tomato paste
- 2 pounds/900g cleaned, chopped spinach or 4 10oz./280 g packages of frozen spinach, thawed and drained
- 1 cup/113g uncooked rice
- 2 sprigs fresh mint or 1 Tbs/ 3g fresh dill, chopped (or more to taste)
- 2.5 cups/236 g hot water
- 1 tsp/6 g kosher salt or 1/2 tsp/3 g table salt
- 1/2 tsp/3 g pepper

Instructions:
1. Heat oil in a large saucepan on medium heat until soft, about 5 minutes.
2. Add tomato paste and rice and cook until tomato paste has darkened and rice is translucent, about 2 minutes. Add spinach to pot and cook off any liquid from the spinach. It seems strange to cook off liquid, then add water, but we need and exact amount of liquid for the rice.
3. Add herbs, salt and pepper, and hot water to pot. Bring to a simmer. Cover pot, reduce the heat to medium-low, and simmer without stirring until rice is cooked and the liquid has been absorbed, about 15-20 minutes.

Chickpea Salad (for sandwiches, oil-free)
Ingredients:
- 15 oz./411g can chickpeas, drained and rinsed
- ¼ cup/13g red onion, diced
- ½ red bell pepper, diced
- 3 Tbs/42g oil-free vegan mayonnaise (see recipe below)
- ½ teaspoon/3g Dijon mustard
- ½ teaspoon/3g garlic powder
- ½ teaspoon/3g onion powder
- salt, to taste
- pepper, to taste
- 1 Tbs fresh dill, chopped
- leafy greens, to serve

Instructions:
1. In a medium mixing bowl, add chickpeas and mash with potato masher until a chunky texture is reached.
2. Add the red onion, red pepper, vegan mayo, Dijon mustard, garlic powder, onion powder, salt, pepper, and dill, and stir until well combined. Store chickpea salad in refrigerator for up to five days. To assemble sandwich, spread mixture onto bread and top with leafy greens of choice.

Shrimp Scampi

Serves 4

Ingredients:
- 4 Tbs/60 ml extra-virgin olive oil
- 4 garlic cloves, minced
- 1/2 cup/118 ml dry white wine, shrimp stock, or vegetable broth
- 3/4 teaspoon/4g kosher salt, or to taste
- pinch crushed red pepper flakes, or to taste
- Freshly ground black pepper
- 1.75 pounds/790g large or extra-large shrimp, shelled
- 1 handful chopped parsley
- Freshly squeezed juice of half a lemon
- Cooked healthy pasta or crusty whole wheat bread

Instructions:
1. In a large skillet, heat olive oil over medium heat.
2. Add garlic and sauté until fragrant, about 1 minute.
3. Add wine or broth, salt, red pepper flakes and plenty of black pepper and bring to a simmer. Let liquid reduce by half, about 2 minutes.
4. Add shrimp and sauté until they just turn pink, 2 to 4 minutes depending upon their size.
5. Stir in the parsley and lemon juice and serve over healthy pasta or accompanied by crusty whole-wheat bread.

- Dips & Dressings -

Oil-Free Vegan Mayonnaise

Ingredients:
- ½ cup / 125ml water
- 1 cup raw unsalted cashews
- 1½ Tbs apple cider vinegar OR lemon juice
- ¾ teaspoon sea salt

Instructions:
1. Soak the cashews in hot water for 20-25 minutes, or in warm water overnight.
2. Drain & rinse cashews, and put into a blender with the rest of the ingedients. Blend until smooth.
3. Can be served imediately, but it's better cold.
4. Keep in a sealed jar in the fridge for up to five days.

Homemade Tofu Dip, Herb-flavor (oil free)

Ingredients:
- 1 block firm Tofu (12 oz / 350g)
- juice of 1 lime or lemon
- handful of chopped fresh herbs (parsley, chives, dill, etc.)
- 2 cloves garlic, minced
- 1 Tbs sugarless Dijon mustard

- 2 Tbs horseradish
- salt & black pepper

Instructions:
1. Put all ingredients in a large bowl
2. Mix with an electric hand-mixer, or in a blender (not too long, so your dip doesn't become a sauce)

Homemade Tofu Dip, Tomato-flavor (oil free)

Ingredients:
- 1 block firm Tofu (12 oz / 350g)
- 50g/1.7oz sun-dried tomatoes, finely chopped
- 1 Tbs tomato paste
- 1 clove garlic, minced
- handful fresh herbs, chopped (chives, parsley, dill)
- salt & pepper

Instructions:
1. Put all ingredients in a large bowl
2. Mix with an electric hand-mixer, or in a blender (not too long, so your dip doesn't become a sauce)

Homemade Tofu Dip, Horseradish-flavor (oil free)

Ingredients:
- 1 block firm Tofu (12 oz / 350g)
- juice of 1 lime or lemon
- 1 Tbs sugarless Dijon mustard
- 3 Tbs horseradish
- 3-4 drops Kikkoman (sugarless) Soy Sauce
- ca. ½ cup oil-free vegetable broth (or a bit more)

Instructions:
1. Put all ingredients in a large bowl
2. Mix with an electric hand-mixer, or in a blender (not too long, so your dip doesn't become a sauce)

Homemade Tofu Dip, Tuna-flavor (oil free)

Ingredients:
- 1 block firm Tofu (12 oz / 350g)
- 1 average-sized can of tuna, in water (not in oil)
- juice of 1 lime or lemon
- 1 Tbs sugarless Dijon mustard
- 1 Tbs sugar-free Ketchup
- salt & pepper
- some fresh dill, chives and parsley, chopped
- garlic powder or 1 clove garlic, minced

Instructions:
1. Put all ingredients in a large bowl
2. Mix with an electric hand-mixer, or in a blender (not too long, so your dip doesn't become a sauce)

Oil-Free Creamy Vegan Dressing

Ingredients:
- 1 ½ cups / 350ml sugar-free Soy (or other Non Dairy) Yogurt
- juice of 1 whole lime
- 2 tsp sugar-free Soy Sauce
- 2 tsp seasoned salt
- 2-3 pinches black pepper
- 2 tsp Dijon mustard
- 5oz / 140g cooked-until-soft cauliflower, chopped
- NOTE: Add different spices/flavors every time you make this dressing, (e.g., turmeric, tomato paste, mint, oregano, thyme, etc.), to create different-flavored dressings.

Instructions:
1. Put all ingredients in a blender and blend until smooth.
2. Store in a sealed jar in the fridge for up to five days.

- Desserts & Snacks -

Tofu-Mousse Dessert, Apple & Cinnamon flavor (oil free)

For 3 or 4 snack-times or portions.

Ingredients:
- 1 block firm Tofu (12 oz / 350g)
- 1 Granny Smith apple, unpeeled and grated
- juice of 1 lime
- cinnamon
- 2-3 dashes liquid Stevia

Instructions:
1. Put all ingredients in a bowl and mix with electric hand-mixer, or blend in a blender until smooth.
2. Divide into 3-4 portions in small cups or bowls, sprinkle with extra cinnamon.
3. Cover and chill in the fridge for several hours, because this dessert is better chilled.

Tofu-Mousse Dessert, Mixed Berries flavor (oil free)

For 3 or 4 snack-times or portions.

Ingredients:
- 1 block firm Tofu (12 oz / 350g)
- 5.2oz / 150g mixed berries, frozen or fresh
- juice of 1 lime
- vanilla paste (to taste)
- 2-3 dashes liquid Stevia

Instructions:
1. Put all ingredients in a blender and blend until smooth.
2. Divide into 3-4 portions in small cups or bowls, top with a few whole berries.
3. Cover and chill in the fridge for several hours, because this dessert is better chilled.

Tofu-Mousse Dessert, Pineapple & Mint flavor (oil free)
For 3 or 4 snack-times or portions.
Ingredients:
- 1 block firm Tofu (12 oz / 350g)
- 5.2oz / 150g fresh pineapple, finely chopped
- juice of 1 lime
- handful of fresh mint-leaves, finely chopped
- 2-3 dashes liquid Stevia

Instructions:
1. Put all ingredients in a blender and blend until smooth.
2. Divide into 3-4 portions in small cups or bowls, top with a mint-leaf and small chunks of pineapple.
3. Cover and chill in the fridge for several hours, because this dessert is better chilled.

Light Iced Coffee (w Non-Dairy or Dairy Milk)
Ingredients:
- Lowfat Milk or Oat Milk (or other sugar-free non-dairy milk; enough to fill a medium-to-large tall glass
- Instant coffee-powder
- 3 ice cubes
- liquid Stevia

Instructions:
1. Mix all ingredients in a blender.
2. Pour into a tall glass, sprinkle with some coffee-powder and enjoy!

Papaya-Watermelon Smoothie
For 2 portions
Ingredients:
- 3 ½ oz / 100g well-ripened papaya (cleaned, peeled, and cut in pieces)
- 7 oz / 200g watermelon
- 2-3 ice cubes
- 1 Tbs lemon-juice

Instructions: Mix all ingredients in a blender; Pour into a tall glass and enjoy!

Strawberry-Kiwi Smoothie
For 2 portions
Ingredients:
- 7 oz / 200g strawberries, frozen or fresh
- 1 kiwi (peeled)
- 1 Granny Smith apple (peeled & cut in pieces)
- several dashes liquid Stevia

Instructions: Mix all ingredients in a blender; Pour into a tall glass and enjoy!

ABOUT THE AUTHOR

Dr. Sr. Vassa Larin, host of the popular, online program, "Coffee with Sister Vassa," is a scholar of Byzantine Liturgy and author of many publications, both scholarly and popular, on Eastern Orthodox spirituality and tradition. Born in Nyack, New York in a devout, Russian Orthodox family, Sister Vassa is now based in Vienna, Austria.

For more on her internationally-acclaimed, online ministry,
visit coffeewithsistervassa.com.

Other books by Sister Vassa Larin:

Lent with Sister Vassa: Reflections for every day of Lent

HealthyFast Lenten Guidebook: Reflections and Meal Plans for Every Day of Lent

Reflections with Morning Coffee: 365 Daily Devotions for Busy People

Tune in to Sister Vassa's inspirational,
weekday audio-podcast, "Morning Coffee,"
and walk with zillions of our subscribers through the Church Year at:

patreon.com/sistervassa

NOTES

NOTES

NOTES

NOTES

LENTEN CALENDAR

(Fasting is mitigated on the feasts of Feb 24/March 9; March 9/22; and March 25/Apr 7)

Sun	Mon	Tues	Wed	Thurs	Fri	Sat
Publican & Pharisee	*Fast-free week*					
Prodigal Son						**Memorial Saturday**
Last Judgment / Meatfare	*Cheesefare Week (no meat)*					**All Ascetical Fathers**
Exile from Paradise	*1st Week of Lent (Great Canon)*	Great Canon	Great Canon	Great Canon		**Miracle of St Theodore**
Sunday of Orthodoxy	*2nd Week*					**Memorial Saturday**
St Gregory Palamas	*3rd Week*					**Memorial Saturday**
Veneration of the Cross	*4th Week*					**Memorial Saturday**
St John of the Ladder	*5th Week*		Great Canon (in the evening)			**Akathist Saturday**
St Mary of Egypt	*6th Week*					**Lazarus Saturday**
Palm Sunday	*Holy & Great Week*			**Holy & Great Thursday**	**Holy & Great Friday**	**Holy & Great Saturday**
Pascha	*Bright Week (fast free)*					

www.ingramcontent.com/pod-product-compliance
Lightning Source LLC
Chambersburg PA
CBHW051357110526
44592CB00023B/2864